Anger Management for Youth:

Stemming Aggression and Violence

Leona L. Eggert

National Educational Service

Bloomington, Indiana   © 1994

Copyright © 1994 by National Educational Service

1252 Loesch Road
P.O. Box 8
Bloomington, IN 47402

Cover design by Joe LaMantia

Printed on recycled paper.

Printed in the United States of America

ISBN 1-879639-29-7

Table of Contents

Table of Contents (continued)

Acknowledgements

I am indebted to scores of young people for their many contributions to the development of this work; most importantly, the first high school student who raged at me about what a "lousy nurse" I was! He helped me face my own need for learning how to respond to anger. Countless other youth challenged me to see beyond their expressions of anger, to learn to respond in a helpful manner, to help them manage their anger in ways less destructive for themselves and others. I also owe much to colleagues who have tested these materials in their work with youth and especially to the Personal Growth Class (PGC) teachers for whom these materials were first developed. The needs of the high-risk youth with whom we worked forced me to put these interventions on paper in order to share the approach with the PGC teachers. Their gracious feedback and untiring efforts in testing the program with high-risk youth moved it from the abstract to the pragmatic. These many contributions, including those of others who have inspired me by their work with youth, make true acknowledgement impossible.

About the Author

Leona L. Eggert, Ph.D., R.N., is currently an Associate Professor of psychosocial nursing at the University of Washington, Seattle. She holds a Ph.D. in Speech Communication, with a focus on interpersonal and small-group communication; an M.A. in parent-child psychosocial nursing and cultural anthropology, and a B.S.N. in nursing. She teaches courses in therapeutic communication and helping relationships, group counseling, and the treatment of substance abuse and psychosocial disabilities.

Dr. Eggert has worked extensively for more than 20 years with adolescents, their parents, and teachers, in schools, community mental health centers, churches, and recreational camping programs. She consults regularly on psychosocial issues related to adolescent health promotion and the evaluation of prevention and intervention programs. She is a child/adolescent psychosocial nurse specialist and a certified school nurse and health educator.

Dr. Eggert is a co-author of *Personal Growth Class Groups: A Leader's Guide* and numerous journal articles pertaining to adolescents. She is Principal Investigator of the Reconnecting At-Risk Research Program. Her research focuses on testing social support models for preventing drug abuse, school dropout, depression and suicide behaviors among high-risk youth; therapeutic communication in helper/client relationships; and the effect of psychosocial risk and protective factors on adolescent development within peer, family, and school contexts. Her current two studies, Reconnecting At-Risk Youth: Drug Users and Potential Dropouts and Preventing Suicide Behaviors Among Vulnerable Youth, received funding for five years (1989-1993) from the National Institute on Drug Abuse and for three years (1990-1993) from the National Institute of Mental Health. This work in testing school-based prevention programs has won awards and currently is being disseminated by the National Institute on Drug Abuse.

Foreword

Anger Management for Youth: Stemming Aggression and Violence is one book which is difficult to hate. In fact, it is almost impossible to have any angry thoughts, feelings, or behaviors as you read through the seven chapters and the five teaching modules. This book, like Truth, has needed to emerge from the chaos of our aggressive society and schools. This is the right book at the right time to deal with the growing amount of aggression by our adolescents.

What excites me is that Dr. Eggert has organized this training material in the most realistic, effortless, and successful way. The focus is to train educational staff anger-management techniques so they can teach small groups of troubled adolescents. What is unusual is the focus on small group instruction versus targeting individual students. Also, it doesn't shy away from the hot topics that schools frequently like to ignore or deny.

The conceptual framework is based on cognitive behavioral theory which is consistent at every level of her intervention with particular attention to the importance of developing group bonding and cohesion among the adolescents involved in this program. In many ways this is like the Positive Peer Culture paradigm except that it's more highly structured and sequential. The adolescent group members are given ample opportunity to define their anger sequence and to learn specific strategies for taking control of their anger responses at home, school, work, and in personal relationships.

This book is destined to be a success in our schools since it not only helps these high-risk students understand their self-defeating behaviors but also it empowers them to learn successful skills which are reinforced by their peer group and staff. This is a valuable book which is easy to love.

— Nicholas J. Long, Ph.D.
Director of the Institute
of Psychoeducational Training

Preface

About This Book

Anger Management for Youth: Stemming Aggression and Violence was written to assist group leaders in teaching groups of adolescents to learn anger-management techniques. The major sections include:

An Introduction to *Anger Management for Youth* for Group Leaders

The Introduction provides a brief history of *Anger Management for Youth*, key concepts about anger and anger management, and description of the model. It also covers specific leader competencies for both the group counseling and skills training approaches that are integrated in *Anger Management for Youth*. The overall program goals, objectives, and content of the modules are described and diagrammed.

Getting Started

The Getting Started chapter gives practical information for starting an *Anger Management for Youth* group. Key considerations and sample activities are provided for getting the group started.

Anger Management for Youth Modules

A chapter is devoted to each module in *Anger Management for Youth: Stemming Aggression and Violence*. Background information and specific group-implementation plans and activities are provided. *Anger Management for Youth* modules are sequenced to provide for group development and anger-management skills training—assessment, skills building within the group, and skills application and transfer beyond the group. See page xi for a diagrammatic overview of the whole *Anger Management for Youth* program.

Monitoring and Check-Back Tools

The Appendix contains a number of tools for helping group participants monitor their progress, stay on track, and celebrate successes.

Who It Is For

This book is written for professionals who work with adolescents and young adults. Educators, counselors, school nurses, health-care workers, and other human service professionals should find this a useful addition to their repertoire of approaches for working with youth.

Material in *Anger Management for Youth* is designed for groups that train youth to improve anger management. It can be used to focus primarily on anger control, *or* it can be integrated into groups with a larger life-skills training or psychoeducational focus. Those with experience working with adolescents will have no difficulty tailoring the modules to fit into an existing counseling group. On the other hand, the novice will benefit from additional reading and preparation in group work with adolescents and young adults before attempting to implement *Anger Management for Youth*.

Anger Management for Youth: Stemming Aggression and Violence was written for use in high schools. However, *Anger Management for Youth* can be adapted easily for diverse practice settings, such as community mental health centers, public health clinics, private practice settings, and juvenile justice detention centers, to name but a few.

The *Anger Management for Youth* session activities can be adapted for a wide range of ages, and they are appropriate for various ethnic groups, because the medium for the sessions calls for "real-life examples" from the particular youth in the group. Ethnic diversity and individual values are welcomed in *Anger Management for Youth*.

How to Use This Book

I suggest that you first read the Introduction and Getting Started chapters which contain important "overview" and "start up" information. Among other information, the Introduction includes leader competencies that are key for successful implementation. and the Getting Started chapter provides key points to consider in getting off to a good start. Next, preview the Background, Implementation Guidelines, and Attachments for each of the modules. An overall diagrammatic plan and content of the modules presented at the end of this preface (page xi) should also help in getting a gestalt of the *Anger Management for Youth* program.

With this overview, you can decide how best to structure the number of sessions for the full training program—that is, how many sessions will be required for your group-training purposes. It is important to note that each module can be (but is not likely to be) covered in just one session. There is enough material here to be spread across 10 or more sessions, depending, for example, on whether your group will meet for one or two hours each session. Alternatively, you can decide how you might integrate the key concepts and activities from each module into an ongoing counseling group.

Prior to the first *Anger Management for Youth* session, it will be useful to thoroughly review the first module, An Introduction to *Anger Management for Youth*. Determine which objectives and activities you intend to cover in each session. The Getting Ready section provides directions for the materials you will need and the things you must do ahead of time. Then work carefully through the Cognitive Preparation approach you plan to use. This is crucial for motivating the youth and "getting off on the right foot." Similar tips for getting ready and cognitive preparation are provided for each module. Finally, the monitoring and "check-back" materials in the Appendix are intended to be integrated and used as indicated throughout the five modules of *Anger Management for Youth*. They serve to reinforce learning, celebrate successes, and prevent relapses.

My best wishes to you as you implement *Anger Management for Youth*. I would be delighted to know how the program works for you in your experiences with youth.

Anger Management for Youth Training Overview

Self-Assessment

1

- Engagement & Motivation
- Cognitive Prep
- Intro to Anger Sequence TTFBC
- Pretest

2

- Review Anger Sequence TTFBC

- Exploring Your Anger Sequence

- Focus on Steps 1-5
  1. What pushes your anger button?
  2. Why does it push your button?
  3. How do you respond *inside* when your anger button is pushed?
     a. Thoughts—self-talk
     b. Feelings/emotional arousal
     c. Physiological arousal
  4. How do you respond *outwardly* when your anger button is pushed?
     a. Behaviorally/physically
     b. Verbally/nonverbally
  5. What are consequences for yourself and other(s) when you "lose your cool" inappropriately?
     a. Thoughts—appraisals, self-talk
     b. Feelings—e.g., self-worth, depression, guilt, etc.
     c. Behaviors—e.g., avoidance, crying, aggression

- Contemplate change—focus on:
  1. What would you like to have happen instead?
  2. What would motivate you to change or to try some alternate responses to anger?

- Transition to learning alternative responses

Skill Building in Group: Appropriate Anger Expressions

3

- Cognitive Prep for:
  1. Training to control anger problems
  2. Review of anger-provoking events: thinking that "fuels the fire!"

- Learning appropriate anger responses for four stages: (1) before, (2) when triggered, (3) during upset, and (4) after

- Focus: Stages 1 and 2:
  1. Inoculations for anger problems: Self-talk rehearsals for:
     - before your button is pushed,
     - when first pushed,
     - when emotions are high, and
     - after being provoked.
  2. Focus on keeping your "cool"
     a. QR relaxation technique
     b. Imagery—individual exercise
     c. Group relaxation exercise

- Transition to next session

4

- Review of anger sequence and

- Focus: Stages 3 and 4:
  3. Coping with arousal
     a. Self-talk/self-instruction
     b. Problem-solving approach
     c. Aappropriate verbal/ nonverbal responses
  4. Playback analysis
     a. When conflict is unresolved
     b. When coping is successful

- Transition to application outside group

Application/Transfer Outside of Group

5

- Review of major triggers and troublemakers

- Focus on:
  1. Taking control
  2. Thought refocusing
  3. Relaxation
  4. Scripts for self-talk
  5. Problem-solving with teachers with friends with antagonists with family

- Focus on:
  1. Rehearsal, experience, and "playback" analysis
  2. Group feedback, support

- Focus on:
  1. Support contracts
  2. Success stories
  3. Certificates, rewards

Monitoring/Check-backs

6

1. TTFBC Check-ins

2. Staying on Track
   - Focus on:
     a. Slips vs. falls
     b. Negative vs. positive approaches
     c. Stumbling blocks
     d. Motivators!

3. Diaries

4. Monthly POMS

5. Check-Backs:
   - Focus on:
     a. Success Stories?
     b. Triggers?
     c. Troublemakers?
     d. Taking control?

6. Certificates; Rewards!

Introduction

I. History of *Anger Management for Youth*

Anger Management for Youth grew out of Reconnecting At-Risk Youth, a school-based program designed to help high school students reconnect with school. The specific purposes of the Reconnecting At-Risk Youth program were to help high-risk students decrease their drug involvement, increase their school performance, and decrease depression and suicide thoughts and behaviors. The program was delivered as an elective high school class offering, called Personal Growth Class (PGC), and used small-group methods within a psychoeducational counseling framework.

The students who participated in PGC were identified as at-risk for potential school dropout. They came to us with significantly greater levels of risk factors and lower levels of protective factors than did the typical high school students in our study. For example, the high-risk youth, as compared to typical high school students, had more negative school experiences, greater drug involvement, more emotional problems, more negative peer pressures, and greater family strain and disruption. High-risk youth also had lower levels of personal resources and less social support from significant people in their networks of friends, family, and school teachers. These high-risk students were not connected with school in positive, productive ways that brought about a sense of success and feelings of self-worth. They did poorly in school, were often suspended from classes, and frequently lost credits. Listening to their comments reveals the pain, anger, unhappiness, and alienation they felt:

> I dread getting up in the morning for school...sometimes it's hard to go to school here because I feel left out a lot. Oh well!

> School has always been awful for me. I totally hate it. I don't think I ever liked school. I'm always getting F's and I hate that....If you want to know the truth, I think a lot about dropping out. I don't need this! People are always picking on me, and I always feel stupid.

> High school sometimes makes me feel physically sick...the social cruelty, arrogance, and disregard of people is

phenomenal. High school belittles you to the point of inability to function.

Anger Management for Youth grew out of the discovery that the high-risk youth with whom we were working endorsed significantly greater problems with anger, perceived stress, and depression on the questionnaire we administered before beginning PGC. This was especially true for those youth who also endorsed higher levels of suicidal thoughts. Again, a sampling of their comments lends support and meaning to the statistical findings from our analysis of their questionnaire responses. The emotional pain is unmistakable.

Rumors! I hate rumors! They cause suicide to some and serious depression to others. If people don't know the facts, they shouldn't say anything. They shouldn't say anything anyway.

Sometimes I feel O.K. at school, a lot of times I feel insecure, and other times I feel really mad or just downright shitty here.

There's so much stress right now. I know it'll be better in just a couple of weeks but now my head just keeps going blank and I have this huge pain inside of me.

There is more stress at home than I can manage. I'm the oldest, and right now everyone is totally out of control. We're stealing from each other and from our mother, and everyone is fighting and yelling.

It's been really rough right now. My girlfriend is 16. She has mass family problems. Her mother is an alcoholic and there is never any money in the house. And her problems are totally overwhelming for her and for me. It's like a never-ending depression.

Anger Management for Youth: Developed in Response to a Need

Prompted by our early study findings in 1989 and personal experiences with these students, we searched the literature for anger management approaches that were suitable for preventive interventions with adolescents in schools and had demonstrated efficacy through carefully designed research studies. Classical works found were those of Bandura (1973, 1959), grounded in a social learning theory, and Novaco (1975), demonstrating the efficacy of stress-inoculation training approaches to the control of anger with adults. These approaches were successfully extended to children and youth (Kaplan, Konecni & Novaco, 1983). Similarly based, aggression replacement training (ART) had reported efficacy with institutionalized adolescents or those posing severe aggressive behaviors in communities (Glick &

Goldstein, 1987) and acting-out delinquents (Goldstein, Glick, *et al.,* 1986); whereas, cognitive and relaxation coping skill interventions produced anger reductions among college students (Deffenbacher, 1988; Hazaleus & Deffenbacher, 1986).

Adding *Anger Management for Youth* to PGC

The problem was clear: many youth in our PGC program had difficulty controlling their anger. The need was evident: skills training in anger management needed to be added to our existing Personal Growth Class curriculum. Thus, *Anger Management for Youth* was developed and adapted from existing effective approaches identified above and tested as a prevention approach with youth at risk of failing or dropping out of high school. The modules in this book were written and integrated into four skills-training units within the PGC program: *self-esteem enhancement, decision making, personal control,* and *interpersonal communication.*

Effectiveness of *Anger Management for Youth*

The good news is that there is some evidence to suggest that *Anger Management for Youth* is effective. When anger-management training was incorporated within the PGC curriculum, experimental tests of its effectiveness revealed that the program worked to help participants control their anger and achieve higher levels of emotional well-being. At program exit and five months later, the participants showed marked decreases in anger-control problems, whereas a control group showed little change. Also at program exit, the participants showed significant decreases in depression, hopelessness, and stress; and these improvements were sustained at a five-month follow-up assessment. Typically these gains were only evident after the anger management module was added to PGC and not before (Eggert, Herting, Thompson & Nicholas, 1992). It is important to note, however, that because *Anger Management for Youth* was embedded within the larger PGC curriculum, gains observed are not likely due to the anger management module alone. It remains to be seen when we evaluate it independently (without being embedded in PGC) if similar improvements are made by youth and sustained over time. Also, hopefully others will evaluate the effectiveness of *Anger Management for Youth;* data on its independent effects across multiple samples would provide a much stronger case than do our current data.

Our evaluations of the program included open-ended responses from the youth. Their comments speak to the helpfulness of the group and provide further evidence of the effectiveness of the program on a more personal level.

It was helpful to be able to come to group and express my feelings when I was stressed out.

What I liked best was talking and getting many different opinions about things...to be able to tell something about my problems without getting yelled at.

If you had concerns or problems, you had a place to express yourself or to release frustration.

It was a good outlet for a lot of emotions and feelings and to let out a lot of compressed anger during crises. I was able to see a little from another person's point of view—how 'they' think (stoners, rocks, nerds, intellectuals, quiets) and what goes on in everybody's life in high school.

II. Conceptual Framework for *Anger Management for Youth*

Anger Control: A Cognitive-Behavioral Perspective

The framework used for conceptualizing anger control was primarily an adaptation of Novaco's work with adults, using an integrative, cognitive-behavioral approach as described by Donald Meichenbaum (1977), Meichenbaum and Deffenbacher (1988), and Goldstein and Pentz (1984). Also built into the program for adolescents were activities adapted from Quick and his colleagues' (1980) program for adolescents, from rational-emotive therapy approaches (e.g., Tosi, 1974; Young, 1974), and from existing conflict-management perspectives (e.g., Kindler, 1988). Recent findings and reviews lend support to this cognitive-behavioral framework (e.g., Deffenbacher & Stark, 1992; Goldstein, Harootunian & Conoley, 1994); support the value of integrating aggression replacement training into a modified positive peer culture group format (e.g., Leeman, Gibbs & Fuller, 1993) as is done in *Anger Management for Youth;* and extend our knowlege of prevention and intervention strategies for youth for assessing and stemming aggression (e.g., Parens, 1993; Furlong & Smith, 1994).

Conceptualizing Anger

Novaco's conceptualization of the complexity of anger indicated a need for a multifaceted approach to address thoughts, feelings, and behaviors. From his perspective, anger is an emotional response to being provoked. The provocation causes us to respond at three levels: at a cognitive level, at a feeling and somatic level, and at a behavioral level. The cognitive response is a result of how we appraise the provocation, the attributions and self-statements that we make about it, and the expectations and images that are conjured up. At a somatic or feeling level, anger is fueled by existing bodily tensions and agitated feelings we might be experiencing. Depending on where we are on the tension continuum—from calm and relaxed to tense and agitated—our anger response varies; it can be exacerbated by existing tensions and, in turn, can escalate the provocation or situation. Behaviorally, according to Novaco, both withdrawal and antagonism contribute to the anger. Withdrawal leaves the instigation unchanged, and antagonistic behavior can escalate the initial provocation and provide further cause for angry thoughts and feelings. Bandura's (1973) social learning perspective provides a similar analysis of anger to Novaco's. These perspectives help us to foster youth's understanding of connections between the original provocation and their thoughts, feelings, and behavior that ensue.

Aggression and Counter-Aggression

Others have added to our understanding of anger from a psychodynamic approach (e.g., Long, 1991). This psychodynamic approach is similar to cognitive-behavioral approaches, but points to the counter-aggressive feelings and behaviors that can result in staff when working with aggressive youth, when our "buttons are pushed" by them. Unless we understand that a youth's aggression and hostility can potentially create aggression in us, and unless we learn not to act out this counter-aggression, we will very likely get locked into a power struggle. Power struggles are unproductive with aggressive youth; there are no winners in this cycle.

For these reasons, it is helpful for the *Anger Management for Youth* leader to cultivate self-awareness about his or her own anger response and to develop a support system. The leader may need help in learning how not to get into power struggles with aggressive youth—in not acting out the anger that may be created internally by a youth's expression of anger.

Also, these youth may try to reject the leader and the group before they get rejected. They may unconsciously try to recreate their familiar experiences with school: failure and turmoil. They need strong leadership delivered calmly and competently to provide a sense of stability. A sense of humor also helps.

Key Concepts about Anger from a Cognitive-Behavioral Perspective

Much of the self-reflection and practice in *Anger Management for Youth* centers on the key concept that when provoked to anger, we respond at three levels. In short, we respond with our thoughts, feelings, and behaviors. Key concepts and definitions (about anger, anger control, and anger-management training) that are woven throughout *Anger Management for Youth* are illustrated on page 17.

III. *Anger Management for Youth*: A Brief Description

Schools, an Ideal Setting for *Anger Management for Youth*

Schools are a logical context for establishing preventive intervention programs like *Anger Management for Youth* (see Bond & Compas, 1989). Schools provide access to a broad range of socializing agents, such as peers, teachers, coaches, and parents. School is where youth often get into fights and are introduced and pressured to use drugs or are reinforced in not using them. So both deviant peer bonding and prosocial bonding occur within this context (Eggert & Nicholas, 1992).

Schools are a major setting where health-promotion programs can be offered to reach young people (Bond & Compas, 1989; Dryfoos, 1991a; Hurrelman, 1990; Stone & Perry, 1990). Schools are a primary place where educators, health professionals, and behavioral scientists can implement and observe the effects of interventions with adolescents in ongoing, systematic ways that can be very cost-effective (See also Dryfoos, 1991b; Eggert, 1990; Eggert, Seyl & Nicholas, 1990; Eggert & Herting, 1993).

The Group Structure

Anger Management for Youth is designed to be delivered within a small-group format. It is intended to have a group leader-student ratio of no more than 1 to 12. This structure permits the integration of small-group methods with life-skills training. *Anger Management for Youth* can be implemented in a school as a regular class for credit, as an independent study option, or as an extracurricular class. Structuring an *Anger Management for Youth* group outside of school also is possible. *Anger Management for Youth* is designed to be adaptable to many settings.

Goal and Objectives

Anger Management for Youth has one major goal for the participants: constructive management of their anger responses. Achieving this goal means making changes in thoughts, feelings, and behavioral responses to provocations that stimulate an anger response. The overall program objectives, directed toward goal achievement, are shown in the box on the next page

---

GOAL: CONSTRUCTIVE MANAGEMENT OF ANGER

Objectives

1. Analyze mood patterns and identify triggers for anger, anxiety, and depression.

2. Set goals for anger management, linking thoughts with feelings and actions.

3. Practice and apply techniques to manage uncontrolled anger and mood swings or emotional spirals.

4. Give and receive support for controlling anger and upward or downward emotional spirals.

5. Monitor anger and other moods, revise goals as needed, celebrate successes, and prevent relapses.

Note that objectives 1 to 3 move from self-assessment and recognition of one's anger sequence to setting goals for change, to building skills in expressing anger constructively, and to applying those skills in real-life settings. Objectives integrated into *Anger Management for Youth* include providing and receiving group support for achieving the goal (#4), and monitoring activities in order to prevent relapses and to celebrate progress and successes (#5). Objectives 4 and 5 are important in that they foster reinforcement of the new behaviors learned in objectives 1 to 3.

Anger Management for Youth is intended to counteract existing aggressive behaviors that create problems for youth in their interpersonal relationships at school, at work, or at home. An underlying belief is that given a supportive, caring environment, aggressive or depressed students can learn the kinds of social and personal skills they need to control their anger responses. A goal of anger-management training is to learn to express anger (or depression) in ways that are less destructive for both self and others. And, as anger-management objectives are met, students repair or build bridges that *reconnect* them with school, family, and friends.

IV. The *Anger Management for Youth* Model: A Psychoeducational Approach

The group-work model for *Anger Management for Youth* is an integration of two submodels: 1) a group support system and 2) a life-skills training approach. For this reason, it is considered "psychoeducational" group work. In this integrated model, group participants experience giving and receiving *support* (in the form of expressed acceptance, belonging, caring) and help (in the form of skills training). This integrated model has its roots in elements of Vorrath and Brendtro's *Positive Peer Culture* (1985), and Schinke and Gilchrist's *Life Skills Counseling With Adolescents* (1984).

The Group Support System

Group bonding and support are the essential medium in the *Anger Management for Youth* model.

The motivating force for behavior change comes from the positive peer-group atmosphere that the leader creates. The support and help received within these interpersonal relationships provide the medium for the skills-training component. It is through these positive and caring relationships that skills training is fostered and program goal achievement is enhanced.

Anger Management for Youth acknowledges youths' primary need for belonging.

To provide the kind of setting where behavioral changes can occur, an essential first step is to meet the students' needs for *belonging,* for being accepted by peers and receiving understanding and help from them. They must feel welcomed and valued and have a good experience in the group, leaving with a sense of having been accepted and understood. One essential element, then, is the support and caring received from the group leader and peers within the group. This develops a sense of belonging or bonding. In turn, this sense of belonging provides the necessary environment in which youth can develop personal control and the power to effect positive change in their lives. The activities in the group sessions nurture bonding and behavior change by encouraging the expression of care and concern among group members. The caring behavior of group members and the group leader communicates the message, *"You are a valuable person; you belong here."*

Students need to be introduced to concepts of group support right at the outset of *Anger Management for Youth*. Group support is the heart of *Anger Management for Youth* in that it sets the pace and stage for subsequent skills training. You may notice that some groups seem to progress much more quickly than others. The difference may be related to differences in their levels of trust, bonding, and group support.

Our participants gave voice to the importance of this support, caring, and group belonging. We consistently got more comments about the importance of this component of the program than about anything else.

> *I liked being able to speak up, the sense of belonging, the support, and even the fights.*

It seemed like everybody really cared and expressed their opinions; and even though I didn't do much talking, I listened and I could relate it to some of the things that were going on in my life.

I liked being able to be as open as I needed or wanted without worrying about whether or not I might get in trouble for my dastardly deeds!

The Life-Skills Training Submodel

Skill is a necessary ingredient for behavioral change.

Group belonging and support is necessary but not sufficient for behavioral change. Whereas group belonging theoretically provides a propitious environment for growth and development, skills training provides the necessary *tools* for change, for being able to think and behave in new ways.

Skills training for dealing with problems or behaviors, such as stress, depression, drug involvement, or difficult interpersonal relationships and uncontrolled anger, is not a new concept or method. It is a very pragmatic approach for working with young people. It is also adaptable. While *Anger Management for Youth* was designed for working with groups, it can be used with individuals, couples, or families.

Categories of skills.

Many of the skills students practice in *Anger Management for Youth* are useful tools in other areas, such as visualization, relaxation, affirmations, self-praise, and group praise. These specific skills can be grouped into four major categories:

Category	Specific Behaviors
Supporting	• Committing to sharing helpful instead of hurtful feedback in group
	• Coaching each other in making positive affirmations
	• Offering help to reverse negative self-talk
	• Taking leadership in directing friends away from self-destructive behaviors
Decision Making	• Targeting a personal goal created through positive visualization exercises
	• Making a goal statement regarding anger control and management training
Problem Solving	• Comparing hurtful vs. helpful feedback
	• Linking thoughts, feelings, and moods
	• Identifying triggers to anger, to depression
	• Exploring self-image and thoughts when feeling angry or depressed
Coping	• Writing and saying affirmations
	• Practicing relaxation techniques
	• Creating positive self-images through visualization
	• Replacing hurtful thoughts with helpful thoughts
	• Exploring healthy ways of coping with personal stressors
	• Applying specific skills to the goal of constructive anger management

Sequential training format.

Skills training in *Anger Management for Youth* follows a sequential format that starts with motivating students to get involved and then moves to making certain that every student is competent in each of the skills before expecting application of the skills in group and real-life situations. The three primary phases are:

1) ***Motivational Preparation,*** which includes introducing the key concepts in such a way that the students know the "what, when, how, and why." This element of skills training is designed to introduce and to motivate, essentially answering the students' questions of "What are we going to do?" "How are we going to do it?" and "Why do it or what's in it for me?"

2) **Skills Building**, which includes activities designed to help the students develop the skills and become knowledgeable and competent in the initial use of the skills. *They can't apply what they don't know how to do.*

3) **Skills Application and Transfer**, which include practice in applying the learned skills to events in the group and, then, applying these competencies to real-life situations outside of the group.

Strategies for *preventing relapse* are incorporated throughout the *Anger Management for Youth* modules. In essence, slips and relapses are prevented by achieving competence and confidence in each step of the skills training sequence.

Figure 1 depicts a more specific "staircase" framework of how the *Anger Management for Youth* model is used to help students achieve the program goal of constructive management of anger responses. The first four essential steps are 1) motivating youth to join the group and get involved; 2) helping them develop awareness of the concepts of anger and anger control; 3) fostering a personal understanding of their current thoughts, feelings, and behaviors in anger-provoking situations; and 4) helping them contemplate change and make the transition to deciding on changes to make. The next four essential steps all relate to taking action, skills building, skills application, and relapse prevention. They are 5) learning and practicing the skills in group; 6) applying the skills in group and then in real-life situations with family, friends, and others; 7) monitoring progress systematically and on a regular basis; and 8) staying successful by getting and giving support to self and others and by contracting for rewards.

Figure 1

CLIMBING THE STAIRS TO SUCCESS
IN *ANGER MANAGEMENT FOR YOUTH*:
TAKING IT ONE STEP AT A TIME

8 Staying Successful
- Rewards: internal/external
- Network support

7 Monitoring Progress: Daily/Weekly
- Check-back activities, diaries
- Coping with anger: habit checks

6 Skills Application to Mood Management
- Taking control, getting support
- Using thought refocusing, self-talk scripts
- Using relaxation & other coping strategies
- Using problem-solving & negotiation skills

5 Skills Building: Learning, Practice, More Practice
- Inoculations against anger problems, learning & practice
- Keeping your cool/QRs, imagery, relaxation practice
- Coping with arousals, learning and practice
- Using play-back analyses, practice, practice, practice

4 Setting Goals: Deciding to Change
- Contemplating change—what would you like to have happen?
- Setting short-term vs. long-term goals for changes

3 Understanding: Personalizing Data
- Discovering what pushes your anger button and why
- Finding out how you respond in different situations
- Discovering what the consequences are for you and others

2 Developing Awareness: Baseline Data
- Pre-test, exploring your anger sequence: TTFBC
  Triggers, Thoughts, Feelings, Behaviors, Consequences
- Linking thoughts, feelings, behaviors

1 Getting Motivated: Getting Started
- Accepting a personal invitation to get involved—*We want you to join and belong*
- Being persuaded to see that problems are an opportunity for change, growth
- Having hope and seeing this as a great chance for helping yourself and others

Like any staircase, one can climb up and down the stairs. Taking a step backwards in *Anger Management for Youth* can be a positive step of relearning, or it can be a "slip" that needs to be recognized and, it is hoped, stopped with only one step backward. However, recognizing the reality of "slips" and knowing that they will happen for everyone is the key approach to preventing relapse. *Anger Management for Youth* includes skills training and group support for pausing to "catch one's breath," rethink one's goals, and then resume the climb.

When skills training is made appealing to youth and relevant to their personal experiences and problems, they respond positively and demonstrate improvements. Again, their comments tell some of the story: what they valued, insights they gained, skills they learned.

> *I'm really glad I got into this group, because I really have enjoyed being a part of it. I know now that in the future when I get mad I can look back and actually see why I'm stressing out.*

> *I learned a lot of valuable communication skills. Like now, before I get mad I'll just kinda stop and do a 'QR' (quieting response)—you know, just kind of relax for a second and think about it and let my anger out. I do that a lot now. I think I'm a better listener now, too.*

> *It helped just to come in and blow off steam and bitch. Also, to hear other people talk about their problems and to observe how they dealt with them.*

V. Group Leader Role

The key to the success of *Anger Management for Youth* is the "delicate dance" between fostering a positive peer-group culture and facilitating skills training: first within the safety of the group and then in other interpersonal relationships with friends, family, and teachers, among others.

It is important that the group leader understands the essential distinction between an *Anger Management for Youth* group and group therapy in a process-oriented group. Facilitating an *Anger Management for Youth* group is a psychoeducational process that combines group-work methods with a skills-training approach. Thus, the leader must be able to use a wide range of peer-group support strategies. The leader also must be thoroughly versed and facile in using experiential learning opportunities within a small-group setting.

There is both an art and a science to leading an *Anger Management for Youth* group. The art is in developing and maintaining constructive and supportive group processes. It also takes artful work to integrate the real-life opportunities for skills training in a group when participants trust and support each other.

Leader Role Competencies for the Group-Support Component

Creating the group-support system calls for the leader to teach, role-model, and reinforce support and caring as the group develops. The leader's role is to ensure that students receive encouragement, nurturing, support, and caring from the leader and from their peers in the group. *Specific group leader competencies* for this component were adapted from Vorrath and Brendtro's *Positive Peer Culture* model and fall into three main categories:

Category	*Specific Leader Behaviors*
1. Motivating the Group— Making Caring Fashionable:	• Positively reinforcing helpful behavior (e.g., as strong, mature)
	• Reinforcing trust and openness in communication
	• Negatively reinforcing harmful behavior (e.g., as weak, destructive)
	• Creating anxiety when students are indifferent to harmful behavior
	• Providing redirection for "caring" behaviors as needed
2. Problem Identification:	• Developing (and maintaining) a format for problem identification (e.g., list of destructive responses to anger)
	• Developing (and maintaining) procedures for problem identification (e.g., agendas, "asking for group time")
	• Reinforcing acknowledgement of problems as "normal" opportunities for change and growth
	• Providing redirection for problem identification as needed
	• Incorporating the participants' issues in the skills training
3. Problem Solving— Reversing Responsibility:	• Referring questions (problem solving) to the group
	• Communicating confidence in students' competence to do what needs to be done to build and maintain a positive peer-culture group

- Conveying a total commitment/belief in the potential of the group

- Involving the group in processing group behavior and progress

- Pointing out the seriousness and harmful nature of negative behavior

- Placing high demands/challenges on the group to deal with problems in a helpful manner

- Providing redirection for problem solving as needed.

Leader Role Competencies for the Skills-Training Component

The skills-training component of the model emphasizes teaching, practicing, and facilitating application of the specific target skills for improving anger control. When students use these skills, they should perceive less stress, greater emotional well-being, and greater self-esteem. *Specific group leader competencies* for this component were adapted from Shinke and Gilchrist's model, *Life Skills Counseling for Adolescents,* and fall into three main categories:

Category	*Specific Behaviors*
1. Motivational Preparation:	• Providing a "cognitive map" of the "what and how" the skills training will involve
	• Motivating students by explaining "what's in it for them," answering the question, "Why bother?"
	• Using persuasive power and role-modeling to get students involved
2. Skills Building:	• Explaining, using concrete examples, manipulative materials, or A.V. aids
	• Involving the group in discussion to identify critical features of the skill
	• Providing for performance demonstration or modeling of the target skill
	• Providing every group member with an opportunity to role play or try out the target skill (or sequence of skills)
	• Role-modeling and guiding constructive feedback to build each group member's confidence and allay anxieties about each member's competence in using the target skills
3. Skills Application and Transfer:	• Using role playing/rehearsals or other simulated practice with members' real-life issues within the group

- Making sure that members are judged by others as being competent in the target skill (skill sequence)

- Contracting with members to perform the target skills in their real-life environments (e.g., with friends, at school, at work, at home, etc.)

- Following-up with members' reports of performance and self-evaluations of skill performance in their environments

- Guiding group problem-solving and constructive feedback for staying successful, dealing with "slips," and preventing relapse.

Integrating the Two Sets of Leader Competencies

The leader needs to be most mindful that the two sets of leader competencies in the model are interwoven during the course of the group's development. It is important to note that these leader competencies facilitate a group to bond initially, to work through any "stormy" phases, to develop a common sense of purpose, and to work together on goal achievement.

Note: The categories of leader competencies in each component go hand-in-hand. That is, the making caring fashionable in the group-support system and motivational preparation in the skills training system go together. Teaching the youth group caring and support skills sets the stage for implementing the next pair of leader competencies, problem identification and skills building. Similarly, once group-process procedures are developed and maintained and the group members have built the necessary target skills, then the problem-solving—reversing responsibility and the skills application leader behaviors can be delivered simultaneously.

One of our group leader's called this integration a "delicate dance" between small group counseling and teaching. As he put it,

> *I know pretty well how to get a group of kids to bond. I had a hard time trying to get the content across without losing them or without sounding absolutely ridiculous to myself and to them. So I'm learning to weave it into our work together so that it is believable, retrievable, and usable.*

This is where art and science come together! And there is nothing more powerful than a competent leader who makes caring fashionable for youth who hunger for genuine love and support. No matter how difficult their problems and obnoxious their behaviors, they are still "kids." And kids need support. They need to learn the skills for managing difficult emotions and interpersonal situations before we can expect them to use these skills.

People *EXPRESS EMOTIONAL UPSETS* of problems in many different ways:

- Some get depressed
- Some get furious, angry
- Some worry all the time
- Some feel worthless, inferior
- Some even have "breakdowns" and consider or threaten suicide
- Some use or abuse drugs
- Some don't try, quit or give up

ANGER is NOT simple annoyance, irritation, disappointment.

ANGER is a combination of discomfort, tenseness, resentment, and frustration.

ANGER is an IMMOBILIZING reaction, experienced when our expectations are not met.

ANGER takes the form of rage, hostility, striking out at others, or even the "silent treatment."

ANGER is a choice, as well as a habit! Like all emotions, it is the result of our thinking!

We FEEL the way we THINK
THINKING produces FEELINGS
FEELINGS generate BEHAVIORS

Because human beings have the unique capacity to think and reason, WE CAN CHANGE HOW WE FEEL.

WE CAN CHANGE HOW WE BEHAVE.

ANGER-MANAGEMENT TRAINING IS NOT
trying to do away with feelings;

rather,

ANGER-MANAGEMENT TRAINING IS
learning to increase appropriate expressions of anger.

ANGER CONTROL

means keeping expressions of anger at a manageable and nondestructive level.

Instead of:	*Rather:*
expressed rage	expressed irritation
verbal abuse	expressed disappointment
attacking or withdrawing	negotiating

Getting Started

I. Start Up Organization

Beginning an *Anger Management for Youth* group involves making decisions, planning ahead, and becoming very familiar with the *Anger Management for Youth* model and content. The Introduction chapter described the *Anger Management for Youth* model and the role responsibilities of the group leader. This chapter covers key points that are important for getting started: identifying, selecting, and inviting the group participants; planning for the first sessions; and other key points to remember in implementing *Anger Management for Youth*. Much of the material in this chapter was adopted from the "Getting Started" chapter in *Personal Growth Class Groups: Leader's Guide* (Eggert, Nicholas, Owen, et al., 1993) and is used here with the authors' permission.

Identifying and Selecting Group Participants

Anger Management for Youth originally was developed for integration into the PGC curriculum which was intended for youth at high risk of dropping out of school. To qualify as a "high-risk youth," a student was identified in one of three ways:

1. From school records, as having

   - Below-average credits earned for their grade level.

   - Placed in the top 25th percentile for days absent per semester.

   - Sliding grades and a GPA of <2.3, or a drop in GPA of 0.7 or more within one semester.

2. From referrals from teachers, school nurses, counselors, attendance secretaries, and administrators as being

   - at "high risk" of school failure *and*

   - meeting one of the criteria in item 1 above

3. From school records as being a prior dropout

Others who have tested the *Anger Management for Youth* program in schools identified students from a list of youth who were recommended for school suspensions because of fighting or acts of violence. *Anger*

Management for Youth was offered as an alternative to school suspension. There are many ways to select a group of youths who will benefit from *Anger Management for Youth.*

Table 1. Checklist for Planning Anger Management for Youth

Scheduling the Group

Place:_____ Room:_____

Day and Time: _____

Length of Sessions:_____

Frequency: _____

People Who Need to Be Informed: (List and date when done)

Names	Date	Names	Date
1._____	_____	3._____	_____
2._____	_____	4._____	_____

Inviting Youth and Parent Notification

_____ Review/develop invitation criteria and script.

_____ Explain the purpose of the group.

_____ Explain the expectations of being a group member.

_____ Explore the youth's feelings and opinions about joining.

_____ Notify parents of youth who have accepted invitation.

_____ Get student and parental written consent if needed.

Anticipate Questions from Youth During the Invitation Process and/or During the First Sessions of the Group; Prepare Responses

_____ Why should I join this group?

_____ Who else will be in the group?

_____ Who decides which students get to join?

_____ How do you know which kids have problems and need this group?

_____ What do you do in the group?

_____ What can kids say in the group?

_____ What about discussing personal problems in the group? (confidentiality?)

_____ Can I bring my friends to the group?

_____ Can I really trust other members in the group?

_____ How will we decide things in the group?

_____ Do I have to come to group each time?

_____ Other: _____

Scheduling the Group and Inviting Participants

Initial planning.

Table 1 provides a checklist of things to consider before beginning the invitation process to *Anger Management for Youth*. One important consideration is to decide on the time of day your group will be offered. If offered in a school setting and as a regular class, you and the school administration should decide when during the school day your group will meet (preferably with input from the potential group participants). Mornings are advantageous, because the group can start the day on a good foot for many of the students. Right before, during, or right after lunch often gives high-risk youth a place, a purpose, and an activity that is "drug free." A mid-day time for the group also has the advantage of helping the students get to their afternoon classes following group, classes they often skip. If the group is an extracurricular offering, then a key factor to consider will be when the desired participants are most likely to attend.

The invitation process.

Students should be invited individually from the pool of eligible students. This invitation is best done in person by you. During the invitation process, you explain the purpose of the group in the most positive terms possible. Use words that the students can understand and that communicate that *Anger Management for Youth* is about belonging to a group that works together and supports each other. Also explain the goals and expectations for the group. It will be useful to work from an invitation script so that all students get a consistently positive approach. Emphasize how this group will be different from typical classroom learning.

In the group you will learn skills to help yourself and your friends. You undoubtedly will have many opportunities to receive help from group members and, also, will be in a position to give help to others in the group. It will be like a form of peer counseling. (See Table 1 for other considerations.)

Next, notify parents of students who have accepted and seek their consent. Again, a personal phone call is recommended. Parental consent serves several purposes. First of all, you have a chance to make contact with the parents and enlist their support in helping their student change. Parental consent also heads off any trouble that may arise from parents getting caught by surprise and feeling that something special was being done with their student. Parental contact also gives the leader an opportunity to model support and begin creating the culture of caring between adolescents and parents.

II. Key Points in Preparing for the First Sessions

Background Reading

Organize the first two sessions of activities in *Anger Management for Youth* with the integrated group work/skills training model clearly in mind. The first two sessions are critical for setting a tone in which the positive peer culture can develop and for motivating the group to achieve the program goal and objectives. The Introduction in this book gives you important information about the goals, objectives, strategies, and leader competencies of *Anger Management for Youth*. In reading the chapters detailing each of the five modules, you should see that work on all the program objectives are initiated in the first sessions.

Physical Space and Materials

The room.

Carefully select the physical space where you will be meeting so that it will be a place that the group can identify as its own. Even if the room is shared with other classes or groups, make wall space, a bulletin board, and storage space available to only the *Anger Management for Youth* group. During the first session, the group can personalize the space with signs and drawings. Arrange chairs or desks in a circle to facilitate group discussion and promote group bonding.

Materials.

Each student will need a small three-ring binder with dividers. Students can organize the handouts and monitoring charts they receive throughout *Anger Management for Youth* by putting them behind the appropriate divider in their notebooks.

Gather supplies, such as a flip-chart stand and paper, colored markers, pencils, Post-it notes, blank stickers, and scrap paper that the group can use for activities. The guide to each module lists materials needed for that particular session.

Leader Objectives

An important aspect of planning ahead is knowing the behavior to be modeled by the leader. In addition to those competencies identified in the Introduction, it will be important for the leader to pay particular attention to the following behaviors in getting started:

1. Model positive attitudes and positive self-esteem.

2. Demonstrate belief and interest in each student and the students as "a group."

3. Show positive regard for each student.

4. Be consistently involved in each student's progress.

5. Coach students to express caring for one another and to develop a positive peer-group culture.

6. Protect students from hurtful communication.

Building a Positive Peer Group

Building a positive peer group begins on Day 1. Activities and discussions in the first session should promote group ownership, trust, and openness. The group first experiences support through the care and concern you show and the communication skills you model as a leader. Particular support processes demonstrated and practiced in the first sessions include:

- Showing care and concern for each other

- Listening to each other

- Praising each other

- Celebrating group successes

- Encouraging participation

- Trusting each other

- Giving helpful feedback

- Negotiating the agenda when someone needs time

During the first session, offer the students an opportunity to bond to the meeting place, to you, and to each other. Good strategies for welcoming students and promoting trust are a circular seating arrangement, snacks, handwritten notes of welcome, and any other rewards you can think of for every positive act they do. This is your opportunity for creating an atmosphere of caring, support, and hope.

Establishing Group Rules and Procedures

Session 1 is also a key time to build group rules for discussion. Involve the group in generating ground rules for how they think they should operate and treat each other. Alternatively, provide them with a sample list that stimulates negotiation and acceptance of their "own rules." The group should agree on "ground rules" similar to the following:

Sample Group Ground Rules

- Claim responsibility for your own feelings: "I feel that..."
- Respect others' opinions; you can agree to disagree.
- Avoid put-downs of yourself and others.
- Ask when you don't understand or need help.
- One person speaks at a time. That means let others finish speaking before you start. No commenting to your neighbor when someone else is talking. Make comments to the entire group.
- No "ganging up" on one person. We are here to help each other.
- Once the group begins, we don't leave the circle or room.
- Criticism should be constructive and directed at the problem being discussed, not the person.
- Follow the issue, keep with the problem being discussed.
- Everything that is discussed in here stays in here, please! Do not talk about what goes on in here or what group members say to other people outside of this group.

Key Concepts in *Anger Management for Youth*

During the first session, students should get a preview of *Anger Management for Youth*. (See Module 1 for the overview and the *Anger Management Trip Map*.) To help provide this preview, it is important to be thoroughly versed in the key concepts in *Anger Management for Youth*. In addition, the key concepts in each module provide a rationale for participating in those particular activities. The purpose of communicating and reinforcing key concepts is to help build understanding and the motivation to practice skills and achieve goals.

Key Concepts Related to the *Anger Management for Youth* Group Support System:

- Personal growth is most likely to occur when we share a little of ourselves and trust in one another.
- Showing care and concern for others enhances feelings of acceptance in the group.
- Meaningful relationships evolve from acceptance of self and others.
- We help friends when we express care and concern and give support.
- Friendships enrich our lives and offer us emotional stability.
- Gaining support means getting information and help from other people. Organizations help us in meeting our goals.

Key Concepts Related to *Anger Management for Youth* Skills Training:

- Feeling stressed, angry, or depressed is our inner reaction to outside events and personal experiences.
- We can learn to be aware of our anger, stress, and depression and can practice strategies to control it.
- Delaying an automatic, emotional response is critical to controlling the emotion.
- We can change the way we feel by changing our unhelpful thinking habits.
- We can regulate our moods and prevent depression by changing our thoughts and feelings about ourselves.
- Viewing relapse simply as a "slip" off the path gives us permission to get back on track and resume efforts toward our initial goals.
- Having a plan of action—self-monitoring, identifying high-risk situations, enlisting a support network, and avoiding lifestyle imbalances—helps to avert a possible relapse.
- Setting specific, realistic goals with identified steps toward action helps maintain motivation over time.
- Feeling good about success as the result of our efforts and abilities and rewarding ourselves helps to boost self-esteem and strengthen motivation and the desire to continue with our goals.

Targeting Program Goals and Objectives

Another major objective of the first session is to create a clear agenda that includes skills training directed to the program goal. While the daily agenda should be negotiated with the group, it always should include the topic that teaches a skill or has the group apply a skill. Formal skills training begins in the first module, during which the program goal and objectives are discussed. Most important, the self-assessment of moods begins in those first sessions.

Remember, the first few sessions are critical for establishing the group behaviors and norms you want carried out throughout the program. Be kind but firm! It is very difficult to regain leadership and persuasive power for motivating "care and concern" once you have lost control. Thus, nip inappropriate behaviors in the bud. Monitoring the group closely in the early phases of the group can help decrease problems of resistance as time goes on.

Monitoring Student Progress

A key ingredient in *Anger Management for Youth* is monitoring student progress, and this begins in the first module. This includes student self-monitoring to recognize and celebrate positive growth and change. Students need to see that they are learning and changing. They may be so discouraged when they come into the group that they do not recognize progress when they see it. Thus the monitoring should be visible and easy to do.

The three-ring binders (or folders) for each student can contain progress reports from the group, from you, and from other teachers. All personalized self-assessments and checklists should be put in the binders. You play an important role in fostering progress by the positive comments you make about the growth you see. It will be important to take time to jot down positive comments and observations in writing so that the students can add these to their binder.

Good resources for helping the students monitor their growth are their parents and, in school, other staff members sympathetic to the program. Enlist the students' parents in the program. Let them know about the positive changes you are seeing and ask them to send you notes of specific positive changes they have observed. Also, you can be instrumental in collecting positive reinforcers for the students by sending notes to their teachers about the changes you see and asking them to send you notes describing similar or other positive changes they have observed. Encourage your students to keep in touch with teachers they like by sending them student or group-made requests for progress reports. This positive feedback should then be added to the students' binders.

Note: The purpose here is to *shower* the youth with positive feedback. They typically have had years of negative feedback and respond positively to large "doses" of positive feedback. We have found that by focusing on positive behaviors, many negative behaviors drop by the wayside without much need for comment.

Video Taping Sessions

Plan to video tape sessions if possible. Decide on the best placement for the equipment in order to focus it only on you for the first time. I highly recommend video taping for two primary reasons:

- for guided self-analysis of your work as a leader, and

- for play-back during the sessions of particular group work.

First, guided self-analysis of your sessions is one of the most powerful learning opportunities for continued personal and professional growth. There is no substitute for using video tapes for this purpose. This self-analysis can be facilitated by focusing the camera on you. Video taping your work can also provide you with an opportunity to seek peer evaluation as desired and when convenient to both parties.

A guided self-analysis tool is provided for this self-evaluation at the end of each module. Making this a regular habit in your group work will provide you with the "observations" you need to assess your progress. If video equipment is not available, I recommend completing the self-analysis immediately after each session when the process and content is still fresh in your mind. Also, asking a peer to be a participant observer can be invaluable. In this case, the group should be forewarned; and again, the explanation should focus on this being for the purpose of evaluating your work as the group leader.

But a word of caution: Be gentle with yourself and find those group leader behaviors of which you are proud, behaviors that reflect the goals of creating a positive, supportive environment, first and foremost. Then assess your progress at integrating skills training. Choose only one or two growth objectives.

A simple explanation to the group for the use of video taping can be straight forward. The purpose is that you desire to monitor your own work as group leader. Just as you are expecting the group to grow and make changes in their lives so, you too, are planning to be accountable for your role as their leader.

Second, if the group also wants to be video taped for purposes of seeing how they are progressing, this can be a wonderful way of focusing their attention on specific behaviors that represent growth. Again, spotlighting the positive is important. My experience is that youth benefit greatly from the process in multiple ways.

But another word of caution: As the group leader you will need to set the tone, take the lead in role modeling positive feedback with specific observations for each youth, and monitor closely that group feedback remains supportive. I also suggest that if particular youth do not want to be videotaped, then their desire can be honored by focusing the camera only on those youth who consent. The primary principle of respecting each youth's wishes can be accommodated without sacrificing the value of video taping. And, of course, the tapes should not be viewed by anyone else without the permission and consent of the group. It may also be necessary in some schools or agencies to obtain prior consent from the youth and parents. But, in general, if the video tapes are used primarily for guided self-analysis and for work within the group, I treat this as a typical educational method for monitoring growth, explaining matter of factly the purposes and that the tapes will be erased after the group.

Students in Crisis

High-risk youth are often in crisis. Some may seem to be in crisis all of the time. It is easy to let these crises dominate the group process and skills training, but that lets the tail wag the dog. The intense emotional needs of the students will get in the way of the skills training. You, as the group leader, and the students need to learn how to keep these crises in perspective. This can be very reassuring to them and contribute to a sense of safety in the group.

Crisis intervention also means connecting students with the appropriate support resources. Know the crisis-intervention resources in your community. When students bring crises to the group, involve the group in determining the appropriate intervention steps. It will be necessary to teach these youth how to seek help and counsel from others both in the school and in the community. Your role may include being an advocate for the student, ensuring a fair hearing.

Involve the group in applying the skills they have learned to the crisis situation. But use good judgment. Do not attempt to have students apply skills to complex problems when they have not yet mastered the target skills in simple situations. You and the group must acquire the skills in each module before you can effectively have the group use these skills to help students cope with their big crises. Avoid pitfalls by enlisting the group's cooperation in practicing the skills with less complex issues before attempting the tough problems. Then make sure you get back to those tough issues when the group is ready for them.

Occasionally you may need to notify administrators, counselors, or even law-enforcement agencies of concerns you have about the student in crisis. This is where having a support system and resources for yourself is helpful.

Keeping Sight of Goals

You and your students are forming a very special learning group. It may be one of the very few positive learning experiences your students currently have. You may get discouraged. They may get discouraged. That is normal. Your job is to keep hope alive amid expressions of hopelessness, thus changing those expressions to ones of hopefulness and personal control.

Ready, Set, Go!

Thoroughly review Module 1, An Introduction to *Anger Management for Youth*. If you are going to spend more than one group session on this material, determine which objectives and activities you intend to cover in each session. Gather the materials you will need, and prepare what must be done ahead of time. Then work through carefully the motivational preparation approach you plan to use. This is crucial for "getting off on the right foot." Finally, integrate the monitoring and "check-back" materials in the Appendix with all *Anger Management for Youth* sessions. They serve to reinforce learning, celebrate successes, and prevent relapses.

If you are *not* incorporating *Anger Management for Youth* into an ongoing skills training group, then I recommend that the primary goals of the first session be to orient the group to each other, the program goals, and you. What follows is a sample start. If you are not comfortable with the activities suggested, then plan something that you can do comfortably and that meets the primary goals of orientation. Beginnings are very important, so always take great care to plan optional strategies so that you can shift easily to something that might work best with the group at that moment.

III. Welcome to *Anger Management for Youth*: A Sample Start

As students gather for their first *Anger Management for Youth* session, they take the beginning steps toward shared group ownership and trust in one another. Day 1 is a time of introductions, to one another and to the goals of *Anger Management for Youth*. The purpose of the activities in this session is to build a positive group image and enhance the self-image of each group member. The session also begins the development of group support, of the value of showing care and concern for self and others. (Concepts, objectives and activities for this session were adapted from plans for the first 10 days in *Personal Growth Class Groups: Leader's Guide* [Eggert, Nicholas, Owen, *et al.,* 1993] with the authors' permission.)

Key Concepts

1. Personal growth is most likely to occur when we share a little of ourselves and trust in one another.

2. Showing care and concern to ourselves and others enhances self-esteem.

3. We can regulate our moods and prevent uncontrolled anger or depression by changing our thoughts and feelings.

Learning Objectives

Students will:

1. Describe themselves, their goals, and challenges.

2. Create ground rules for promoting care and concern in group.

3. Practice using a mood diary to monitor feelings and moods.

4. Understand the purposes of the group and get a big picture of what lies ahead.

Preparations

1. Review this session. Review and select from Module 1 the motivational preparation you will use when you present an overview of *Anger Management for Youth*.

2. Arrange chairs in a circle.

3. Copy the three key concepts for the day on the flip chart in large print.

4. Copy sample interview questions on the flip chart.

5. Make copies of Anger Management for Youth and the "Mood Diary" for each student (pages 39 & 40).

6. Make a poster-size copy of the "Anger Management Trip Map" from Module 1 and a master copy for each student (pages 54-55).

7. Acquire a three-ring *Anger Management for Youth* binder for each student.

8. Make copies (one for each student) of any other activities adopted here from Module 1, Introduction to *Anger Management for Youth.*

9. Make arrangements to have the session video taped, if possible.

Materials

1. Flip chart, markers.

2. Blank bookmarks, colored pencils, markers, Post-it notes.

3. Copies of all handouts for each student and posters (see above preparations).

4. Treats (cake, cookies, doughnuts, juice). Make or buy treats to celebrate Day 1 of *Anger Management for Youth.*

   • One option is to make cookies that include a self-esteem enhancement affirmation that you have prepared and put in each (like a fortune cookie). Each person then reads aloud their "fortune" during treat time.

   • Another option is to buy or make a birthday cake to celebrate everyone's *Anger Management for Youth* "birthday" on Day 1.

5. Video equipment.

Introduction

Welcome Students

1. Welcome students by telling them that you are really pleased that each one decided to join *Anger Management for Youth.* Express your confidence that the group will work well together. Be persuasive. Emphasize that today marks new beginnings for all:

   Beginning to share group ownership.

   Beginning to trust one another.

   Beginning to learn more about our moods.

   To celebrate these new beginnings and the "birthday" of *Anger Management for Youth,* invite students to help themselves to treats.

Introduce Key Concepts

2. In your own words, explain the purpose of this introduction to *Anger Management for Youth* as expressed in the key concepts for today (which you have printed on the flip chart).

Preview

3. Tell students that beginning to trust each other involves taking some risks. The first risk today is what we choose to share about ourselves during introductions.

Activities

Negotiate Agenda

4. Emphasize that you will be making many shared decisions in the group throughout the *Anger Management for Youth* sessions.

We can start now by deciding how we'd like to do introductions.

Provide Options

5. Introduce the options below and ask for other ideas. At the same time, show them the sample questions (see below) for introductions that you have written on the flip chart. Here are the options:

Option 1

Go around the circle and introduce yourselves. Tell us a little bit about yourself in relation to each of the sample interview questions on the flip chart.

Option 2

Work in pairs. First, spend about 5 minutes listening to each other's responses to the sample questions. Second, go around the circle and introduce each other to the group.

Do you have other ideas that you would like to try?

(Note: Option 2 is less threatening for those who are shy, and it also has the advantage of letting everyone begin to talk in the group. For these reasons, it is my preference.)

Group Discusses

6. After the group members have decided how they would like to do the introductions, ask if they have additional interview questions that they would like to add to the list. Ask for a volunteer (or ask a student who looks willing) to record the students' additional

questions on the flip chart, rather than doing the recording yourself. This helps the students start taking ownership of the group.

Sample Introduction Questions

- *What words best describe you?*

- *What are one or two things you do that you are really proud of?*

- *What are one or two key reasons you joined the group?*

- *What are one or two expectations that you have coming into this group (for example, what would you like to see happen for you in this experience)?*

Group Works on Task

7. If you are using option 1 for introductions, give students time to jot down some ideas for their introductions. Model working silently on jotting down ideas for your own introduction. Monitor the group, and request that they work silently on the task for a few minutes.

   If you are using option 2, give students 5 to 10 minutes to interview each other. Assign students to the pairs e.g., those sitting beside each other or those sitting directly across from each other).

Group Shares

8. Participate in the introductions, modeling appropriate risk-taking. This may be one of those times when it is wise for you to go first in order to model appropriate and expected behavior. Intervene if some students seem to be getting short-changed, and draw them out sensitively. If option 2 is used, an extension is to ask each student if they would like to add anything to their partner's introduction of them.

   Thank students for sharing, for taking the first step toward trusting one another, and for getting to know each other.

   Ask the students:

What similarities are you hearing in strengths, reasons for joining the group, and expectations for the group from what has been shared? (Open answers.)

Pass out Notebooks

9. Pass out notebooks. Explain that this is a "gift"—and it will become a means of collecting treasures from their *Anger Management for Youth* experience. Explain that each week they will put additional "valuables" in their binder. Today, you are starting with one of the most valuable!

Pass out *Anger Management for Youth* Handout

Ask students to fill in the seating chart on the sheet (see page 39). Point out the program goals in the center, and tell students that the group will work on these goals over the life of *Anger Management for Youth*. Tell students to notice the beliefs about group support at the bottom of the sheet.

Tell students that one of the most important things the group will do together is to be supportive of each other. This also can be called caring about and encouraging each other.

Today, we'll be working on the goal of showing care and concern for one another.

Group Brainstorms

Brainstorm together what care and concern sound and feel like. Start with the list on the handout. Tell students that another group of teenagers with whom you have worked came up with this list.

How does the list feel like care and concern to you? (Open answers)

What would you change on this list?

(Allow students to brainstorm, discuss, add, or delete items. Have someone else be the recorder, and record any additions on the flip chart).

Ask students to think of various issues, difficult or pleasant, that might come up in group. For example:

- Broke up with girlfriend/boyfriend
- Made the team
- Totalled the car
- Aced a test

Group Works in Pairs

10. Students divide into pairs to discuss one of the issues (or make up their own). The pairs prepare two brief lists of helpful (supportive) and hurtful ("put-down") responses to the issue. (Optional: Have pairs prepare a role-play of the helpful response. Note: No role-playing of the "put-downs," because this just reinforces them in the group.)

Group Shares

11. Each pair presents their lists of helpful versus hurtful responses. Have a recorder write down students' examples in two columns labeled "Helpful" and "Hurtful" on the flip chart. Ask for volunteers to present the role-plays of a helpful response. Have the rest of the group give (only positive) feedback after each role-play.

    Guide group feedback by asking:

How does a helpful or supportive comment affect your self-esteem (the way you feel about yourself)? (Builds self-esteem.)

How does a hurtful comment or put-down affect your self-esteem? (Weakens self-esteem.)

How can talking about our feelings be helpful? (Open answers. Possible answers: Relieves stress, helps us understand our feelings, helps when someone really listens and understands—this means a lot!)

With what kind of person would you be likely to share your feelings? (Open answers. Possible answers: A friend, someone who listens and does not criticize, someone who can be trusted.)

    Explain that the group can show that same kind of care and concern to each other as they talk about feelings and moods.

Introduce Key Concept

12. Explain that self-esteem is affected by both what others say about us and by what we say to ourselves.

    Ask students:

Do you ever put yourself down? If so, in what ways? (Open answers. Share your own experiences with negative self-talk.)

    Tell students:

We may be less conscious of the negative messages we give to ourselves than of what other people say to us. Nonetheless, these negative self-messages influence how we feel about ourselves.

Preview

13. Give students a brief summary of the ways the group will work to change negative self-messages: thought refocusing, visualization, affirmations. Explain that by the end of the session today, they will see how some of these techniques work.

Group Shares

14. Give each student several notes from a "Post-It" pad. Tell students to think of various moods they have experienced in the past week (for example, happy, sad, frustrated, angry, energetic, bored). Have students write one mood per note, then read and describe what they wrote. (An option is to have students stick the notes on themselves, thus "owning" the feelings.)

Problem Identification (Optional)

15. Give each student two sheets of paper. On one sheet, students stick moods they consider normal. Emphasize that "normal" might include a range of emotions. On the other sheet, students stick moods that have somehow been hurtful to them. These may be moods that they would like to control better. Discuss the possibility that a mood might appear on both pages. For example, anger is normal and often helpful, but it also can be uncontrolled and hurtful. (If students have stuck the notes on themselves, they can peel off the hurtful moods and put them on a piece of paper.) Have students share their lists.

Preview, Inspire

16. Tell students that in the group they will work to get "unstuck" from hurtful moods and to experience more helpful moods. They will begin by monitoring moods and looking for patterns and causes of moods.

Pass out Mood Diary

17. Pass out copies of the Mood Diary (see page 40). Have students write their names and starting date on the sheet.

Instruct

Explain how the diary works by telling students:

The numbers represent a range of feelings or moods. To assign a number to a mood, first think of the saddest you've ever felt. Write that example at the bottom of the page and give that mood a 1 if you think it would be impossible to feel any worse. If you might be able to feel worse, give it a 2 or 3. Now think of the happiest you've ever felt. Write that example at the bottom of the page and give that mood a 10, or an 8 or 9 if you think you could feel even better.

Now compare how you feel today with these two feelings. Give your mood a number and write it in the box for today. Circle the corresponding number above the box.

Group Shares

Ask students to share their ratings for their mood today (anyone can "pass" if they would rather not share). Record the average rating on the flip chart and point out the general level of the group's mood scores today.

Show students how they can connect the numbers to show how their moods have changed during the week. Have students put the diary in their notebook under "Mood." Alternatively, have students fold it and put it in their wallets. Ask them to record their mood daily for the next week. At the end of a week, they will be asked to share their results.

Motivational Prep

19. See this section in Module 1. Select the option of your choice and implement it, giving the students a preview of how *Anger Management for Youth* will help them and the payoffs for getting involved.

Pass out the Anger Management Trip Map (see pages 54-55) and use the poster of it to explain, in your own words and with enthusiasm, what is in store for the group. Emphasize that you will do everything possible to make it appealing and very worthwhile.

Wrap It Up

20. Summarize and personalize the insights gained and the observations of positive things you noticed and appreciated. Thank the group for their fine work. For example,

Wow! You did good work today! Thank you. I think we're off to a good start! But, I'm also curious about what you think.

Leader Homework

Ask students:

What would you like to learn more about related to today's session?

You will research their questions and put together a little information newsletter answering their questions. Pass out pieces of paper for students to write questions to be answered in the newsletter.

Thank students again for their positive participation, caring, and support. Tell them you look forward to seeing them again on _____ (name the day of the next group session).

———

Check-Back Activities

1. Prepare for follow-up of the Mood Diary assignment in the next group session.

2. Prepare the newsletter with answers to students' questions.

3. Follow-up on any promises you made to the group.

4. Jot down notes for yourself about each student's expectations for the group, reasons they joined the group, and strengths they shared. Study and be prepared to reveal your recall of these importance pieces of information during the ensuing sessions. This is one very concrete way you have of demonstrating your genuine interest, involvement, and regard for each student.

Self-Praise

Give yourself a pat on the back! You did it! You're off and rolling.

Self-Analysis

Play back the videotaped recording of the group session. Review the list of leader competencies for fostering group support and skills training. Make a list of those you saw yourself implement, and give yourself another pat on the back! Now, identify one or two growth objectives that you would like to work on during the next group session.

Repeat this self-analysis after each group session. If you do not have access to video equipment, the self-analysis should take place as soon as possible after the session. Guided self-analysis is one of the most powerful learning opportunities and avenues for continued personal and professional growth.

ANGER MANAGEMENT FOR YOUTH

The purpose of *Anger Management for Youth* is to accomplish the goals listed in the center of this page. Each and every group member plays a big part in the group's achievement of these goals. Write your name and the names of the group members in the boxes surrounding the goal circle.

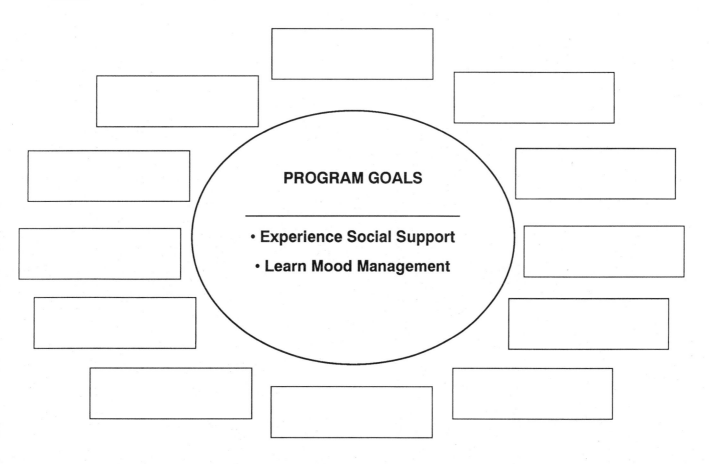

PROGRAM GOALS

- **Experience Social Support**
- **Learn Mood Management**

Our Group Believes that
Care and Concern Are:

1. Listening to each other.
2. Giving helpful feedback.
3. Telling each other we care and are concerned for them.
4. Praising each other.
5. Celebrating group successes.
6. Encouraging participation.
7. Trusting each other!

MOOD DIARY

My Daily Mood

Your Name_____   Starting_____

Sun	Mon	Tues	Wed	Thurs	Fri	Sat

Sun	Mon	Tues	Wed	Thurs	Fri	Sat

Sun	Mon	Tues	Wed	Thurs	Fri	Sat

Sun	Mon	Tues	Wed	Thurs	Fri	Sat

Sun	Mon	Tues	Wed	Thurs	Fri	Sat

Sun	Mon	Tues	Wed	Thurs	Fri	Sat

Sun	Mon	Tues	Wed	Thurs	Fri	Sat

Sun	Mon	Tues	Wed	Thurs	Fri	Sat

Please use the scale below and circle the appropriate number above that day's date. Connect the numbers to see how your mood has changed.

Very Sad				Normal Mood				Very Happy	
1	2	3	4	5	6	7	8	9	10

Sad Example _____   Happy Example _____

Introduction to *Anger Management for Youth*

I. Background

Brief Description of the Module

This module introduces *Anger Management for Youth*, Managing Anger Skills Training. It is designed to prepare the group participants for the entire anger-management program. The overall purpose is to engage and motivate students to:

1. Explore the topic of anger and anger management,

2. Understand what anger management is and is not,

3. Understand the benefits of learning anger management.

Included in this introductory module is a pretest of students' mood states, including anger, depression, anxiety, vigor, fatigue, and confusion. This serves both to introduce the students to their mood states and to provide them and the leader with a baseline of their individual mood states when they entered the program.

Learning Objectives

Students will:

1. Be introduced to a general outline of anger-management training.

2. Rate their levels of anger responses and compare them to others.

3. Understand the anger sequence: controlled *vs.* uncontrolled.

4. Be motivated to engage in self-assessment of their personal anger sequence.

Training Level

(X indicates those that apply to this module)

<u>X</u> Skills Assessment (pre)   ___ Skills Acquisition
___ Skills Assessment (post)   ___ Skills Application
<u>X</u> Skills Monitoring/Check-Backs

Leader Strategies

An important aspect of introducing *Anger Management for Youth* and motivating the students to engage in this program of behavior change is the behavior modeled by the group leader. It will be important for the leader to:

- model positive attitudes about learning anger management.

- demonstrate a belief and interest in each student and in the students as a group.

- show positive regard for the students.

- be consistently involved in their progress.

- coach students to express caring for one another and to develop a positive peer-group culture.

- protect students from hurtful communication.

In addition to encouraging and fostering a culture of caring within the group, specific strategies the leader is expected to use in this module are:

_X_ Instruction	___ Game
_X_ Modeling	_X_ Questionnaire/Scale
_X_ Group Discussion	___ Group Exercise
___ Group Practice	___ Role Play
___ Indiv/Dyad Practice	___ Real-Life Assignment
_X_ Homework	___ Other: _____

Attachments

1. Comparison of Feelings/Experiences (study results) (page 53)

2. Anger-Management Trip Map (pages 54-55)

3. Anger-Management Training: some definitions (page 56)

4. The Uncontrolled Anger Sequence (overhead master and discussion outline) (pages 57-59)

5. Major Themes (page 60)

6. "Today...I discovered that I ..." (page 62)

7. Scoring the POMS (page 63)

Leader Preparations

Materials needed and things to do ahead of time include:

1. Handouts/Teacher Guides

    a. Comparison of Feelings/Experiences (study results) (make a copy for each student)

    b. Cartoons/"Dear Abby" or teen advice column letters (collect and reproduce yourself if you use this approach)

    c. The Uncontrolled Anger Sequence (discussion outline)

2. Posters, Overheads to Make (or Handouts)

    a. Anger-Management Trip Map (enlarge and post)

    b. Some definitions (enlarge and post, or copy for each student)

    c. The Uncontrolled Anger Sequence (make copy for each student's notebook)

    d. How do you respond to anger? (enlarge and post) (make copy for each student...collect results)

    e. Major Themes (make copy for each student's notebook)

    f. "Today...I discovered that I..." (enlarge and post)

3. Pretests

    Decide on one of the following tools to use as a pretest (and again as a post-test at the end of the program). Obtain the tools well in advance in order to decide on your preference, study them, and learn how to use them.

    a. POMS test and POMS Profile Form—a copy of each for each student. (Note: these are copyrighted and must be purchased from the publisher—see page 156 for the source.) If using the POMS, also make a copy of Scoring the POMS, page 63.

    b. Or, use the *Symptoms of Stress Inventory* (the SOS) and its guide to scoring and interpretation (make copies of each for each student) (Note: see page 156 for the source.)

    c. Or use "My Typical Anger Triggers & Troublemakers" in the Appendix (page 141).

    The advantage of the POMS is that it is brief and has well-established norms. Another advantage is that it measures more than just anger—i.e., tension, depression, anger, vigor, fatigue and confusion/uncertainty. The disadvantage of the POMS is that it needs to be purchased.

The SOS has all the same advantages as the POMS with the added advantage of being available at no cost. The disadvantage is that it takes somewhat longer to administer and score.

The advantage of using "My Typical Anger Triggers & Troublemakers" in the Appendix is that it is simple and available. The disadvantages, however, are that there are no scoring methods or norms to use as a basis for comparison, and it only addresses anger.

My recommendation is to use either the POMS or the SOS for pre- and post-tests and to use "My Typical Anger Triggers & Troublemakers" for process evaluations and monitoring during the course of the program.

4. Set up equipment for video taping session.

Implementation Guidelines

Part I: Motivational Preparation

Skills-training group sessions include motivating behavior change by providing students with the "what, how, and why." These are persuasive strategies that, theoretically, should motivate the students to get involved. The key is that whatever cognitive preparation is used, it should be culturally relevant to the students involved. It also must fit the style of the leader and be an approach the leader is comfortable with.

It is important to remember that this module provides the *cognitive preparation* for the entire *Anger Management for Youth* program. Most of the activities within this module are designed to engage the students, motivate them to contemplate how they deal with anger, and persuade them to learn alternative anger expressions with guaranteed payoffs for them.

Here are some options for openers that try to accomplish the above goal and cover the questions that will be in the mind of the students:

- "What's in it for me?" or "Why bother?"

- "What are we going to do?"

- "How are we going to do it?"

There certainly will be other "openers" that might work better with your particular group of students. For example, you might want to start with the pretest, discuss and compare students' profiles, and then go from there with the other activities, leaving the rationale and program overview to the end of the first session in this module, as a transition into the next session.

1. Introduction Options or "Openers":

I'd like you to look at this graph (see "Comparison of Feelings"). *It shows results from our study of how kids in PGC classes (Group 1) compare with most kids in school (Group 2). This information includes kids from all four high schools. Notice that PGC kids generally feel significantly more depressed or angry and have more thoughts of suicide. This is a problem! It is something we need to work on and something I want to help you with.*

OR

Did you know that most relationships (friendships, marriages, even brief acquaintances and working relationships) get into trouble because people don't know how to deal with disagreements and then let their anger get out of control?

Most of us have real problems in dealing with anger: Listen to this! (or Look at this!) (Use examples from "Dear Abby," teen advice columns, comic strips, or whatever, to illustrate your story.)

How many of you have problems controlling your anger? Or knowing how to express it? Or knowing how to respond when someone else blows up at you? You're not alone! Anger management is a life skill we all need to learn. We're going to share our experiences and learn this together!

OR

You know, _____ just presented a personal problem that really shows us how getting angry and "losing our cool" can get us into more hot water than we ever dreamed of. He's (she's) not alone! We all get our buttons pushed at times, and how we respond can end up with some pretty bad consequences.

So, now that we've had a chance to help him (her) with his (her) specific problem, it seems like a good time to start some work on anger management, something that will help all of us.

2. Why Anger Management Training?

Anger is an emotion that is triggered by all kinds of things that provoke us. Each of us is unique; what provokes one doesn't necessarily provoke another.

Getting angry to the point of losing control is unhealthy in many ways. It's hurtful and can have long-lasting, damaging effects. Let me explain:

What usually happens when we get angry is that we respond somewhere between two extremes:

WITHDRAW——————————————————————ATTACK

Both of these extremes can result in anger-control problems that end up hurting us:

When we withdraw, we remain angry and "stew"; this can lead to feeling more angry and depressed. In fact, one definition of depression is anger turned inward! How does this hurt us? This is damaging to ourselves; it hurts us inside, emotionally and physically (for example, we may suffer headaches, stomachaches, tension, maybe even ulcers, etc.).

When we attack, what usually happens? We get even more angry and may hurl abuse (words and/or fists). This gets us into more trouble, for example:

  • *here at school (suspensions, loss of classes, etc.);*

  • *at home (getting grounded, etc.);*

  • *with friends (fights, hurt feelings, loss of friend);*

  • *at work (getting fired).*

So withdrawing or attacking rarely settles the problem!

3. What Are We Going to Do?

We're about to go on a trip where the final destination will be anger control. (Use the Anger-Management Trip Map to make your points.)

By the time we complete this trip, you'll know a lot about your anger sequence. You also will know new skills or techniques for expressing anger in a way that keeps you out of trouble (inside yourself and with others).

We're going to learn two big things:

a) *Your personal anger sequence:*

   What pushes your button.

   What you do when it gets pushed.

   Why does it get pushed.

   What the consequences are.

b) *Various ways of expressing anger that save "face" for you and the other person or persons in the scene.*

As you know, learning new skills and habits can be rough sometimes. I know this, too, and that's why I'm here for you and why we're here for each other.

This is another one of those life problems that's an opportunity for "personal growth." So, this is going to be a team effort between all of us. Together, we can make this pay off in all kinds of ways:

- *with each other here in the group,*

- *in your negotiations with teachers,*

- *at home,*

- *with your "antagonists," and,*

- *most important, with your friends!*

I've got some of the best proven strategies that will help us learn to manage anger and express it appropriately. This is a life skill that we just can't do without!

4. How Are We Going to Do It?

Here's what I propose: (Refer to Anger-Management Trip Map)

- *That we spend some time on this each day this week—on bite-size pieces.*

- *That we start now at the beginning: the pretest and then the anger sequence.*

- *In our next session, we'll move into exploring our own personal anger sequence.*

- *This will get us ready to start learning some new techniques, practicing them with each other here in group, and helping each other with feedback on how we're doing.*

- *Then we'll continue practicing in group all semester, as well as trying out the skills in situations outside of the group (starting with easy ones first to rack up some successes and build our confidence)!*

For those of you who already deal with anger successfully, we'll look to you for ideas and coaching. For those of us who usually blow our cool and let our anger get us into trouble, we're in for some worthwhile challenges!

So, to summarize, as a first step we'll learn more about our own anger. Then we'll move into skills training—learning how to express anger in mature ways! How does that sound? Any questions? Ready to start the trip?

Part II. Learning Activities/Process Guidelines:

1. Administer the Pretest, Giving Directions and Explaining the Purpose

As a first step on our journey toward anger management, completing this short quiz that's called the POMS (or the SOS if that is what you have chosen to use). This tool taps some of the emotions, feelings and thoughts we are dealing with. We will be able to compare our results with those of lots of other people who have completed this tool. We will also use the results in taking the next steps.

Distribute the POMS (or the SOS) and have students complete it. When they have finished, distribute the "POMS Profile Form" and "Scoring the POMS" (page 63) (or similar forms and directions provided with the SOS) to each student Explain how to score their tests and plot totals on the profile form.

Have students share their individual scores especially on *anger and depression,* recording each person's results on a piece of butcher paper. *Purpose:* to discover each person's unique responses and discover the "group profile"—making public to what extent these emotions are problematic for group participants.

Be prepared to go first to engage in and model the same level of self-disclosure you expect from the students. Interpret the scores, using your own results as an example. Answer any questions students have.

It is a good idea at this point to introduce the notion of doing the POMS periodically (for example, every other session) to compare progress made on moods over time.

Your personalized POMS (or SOS) profile should tell you something about yourself and the extent of the feelings you're currently coping with. These may be some of the feelings that have stood in the way of success in school, decreasing drug involvement, getting along with your friends, and so forth. The anger score will tell you the extent of this emotion, but it doesn't tell you what triggers it or what you do with it, does it?

That's what comes next. (Refer to the posted Anger-Management Trip Map to explain the next steps.) Use as a transition to a group discussion of the anger sequence.

2. Group Discussion

Let's try to answer some general questions. This will help us the next time when we start exploring our unique styles and personal obstacles to appropriate anger expressions.

Let's look at some definitions first.

Handout and discuss Anger-Management Training: Some Definitions.

Lead group in discussion (see Uncontrolled Anger Sequence Discussion Outline on page 58). Record students' responses on blackboard, flip chart, or overhead. (After this session, type their responses into an outline form for use in the next group session.)

Part III: Wrapping It Up

1. Summarize, Promote Insight, Personalize

Summarize with *Major Themes* or from students' generated responses.

Use positive feedback and promote insight.

Wow! You did good work today! Thank you. I think we're off to a good start! But I'm also curious about what you think. Would you be willing to finish any one of these statements?

(See the Today...I discovered that I.... poster.) Go around the circle, and give each student an opportunity to respond. Remember their responses.

2. Promote "Taking It Away!"

(Homework, transfer activity assignments)

Between now and our next session, please think about a situation when you got very angry. Start to think about the sequence.

TTFBC: What was the Trigger, your Thoughts, your Feelings, your Behaviors, and the Consequences?

We'll explore personal triggers and anger sequences during our next session.

Part IV: Monitoring/Check-Back Activities

For the next group session, prepare a list of the students' responses to TTFBC generated from group discussion.

Jot down notes on each student's response about what he or she discovered today. Be prepared to integrate this material in specific, positive ways to demonstrate your recall and understanding of the students' progress.

List the other things you want to remember for the next session:

_____

_____

_____

_____

_____

_____

_____

_____

Guided Self-Analysis

Review the videotape of your group session.

Using the lists of Leader Competencies from Chapter 1, complete the following:

Leader Competencies for Fostering the Group-Support System

Examples of strengths in fostering group support I observed were:

1. _____

2. _____

3. _____

4. _____

5. _____

A growth objective to work on next time is:

_____

_____

Leader Competencies for Fostering the Skills-Training Component

Examples of strengths in skills training I observed were:

1. _____

2. _____

3. _____

4. _____

5. _____

A growth objective to work on next time is:

_____

_____

COMPARISONS OF FEELINGS/EXPERIENCES

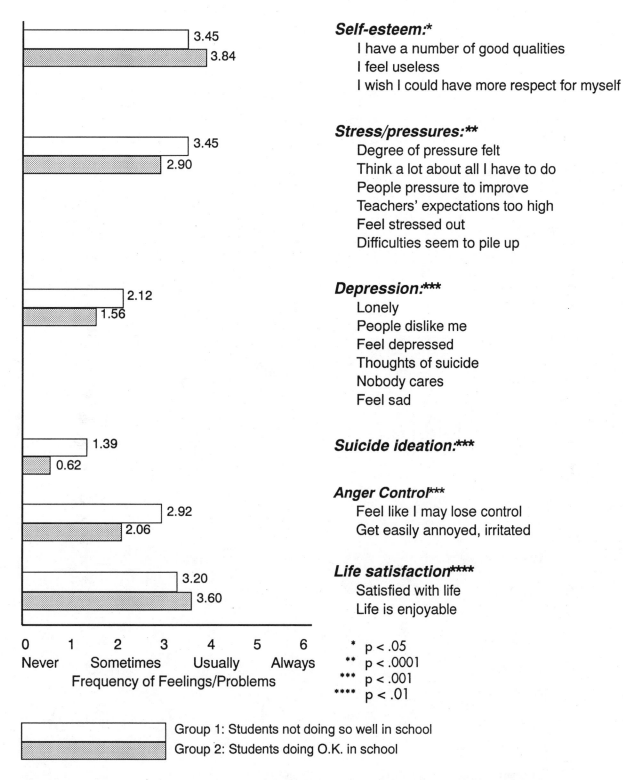

Self-esteem:*
    I have a number of good qualities
    I feel useless
    I wish I could have more respect for myself

Stress/pressures:**
    Degree of pressure felt
    Think a lot about all I have to do
    People pressure to improve
    Teachers' expectations too high
    Feel stressed out
    Difficulties seem to pile up

Depression:***
    Lonely
    People dislike me
    Feel depressed
    Thoughts of suicide
    Nobody cares
    Feel sad

Suicide ideation:***

Anger Control***
    Feel like I may lose control
    Get easily annoyed, irritated

Life satisfaction***
    Satisfied with life
    Life is enjoyable

Chart values:
- Self-esteem: 3.45 / 3.84
- Stress/pressures: 3.45 / 2.90
- Depression: 2.12 / 1.56
- Suicide ideation: 1.39 / 0.62
- Anger Control: 2.92 / 2.06
- Life satisfaction: 3.20 / 3.60

Axis: 0 1 2 3 4 5 6
Never   Sometimes   Usually   Always
Frequency of Feelings/Problems

* $p < .05$
** $p < .0001$
*** $p < .001$
**** $p < .01$

Group 1: Students not doing so well in school
Group 2: Students doing O.K. in school

SUMMARY: The above shows that Group 1 students differ from Group 2 students in feeling more stressed/pressured, depressed, and angry and having more thoughts about suicide. Also, Group 1 youth have less satisfaction and lower self-esteem than do Group 2 students.

AN ANGER-MANAGEMENT TRIP MAP

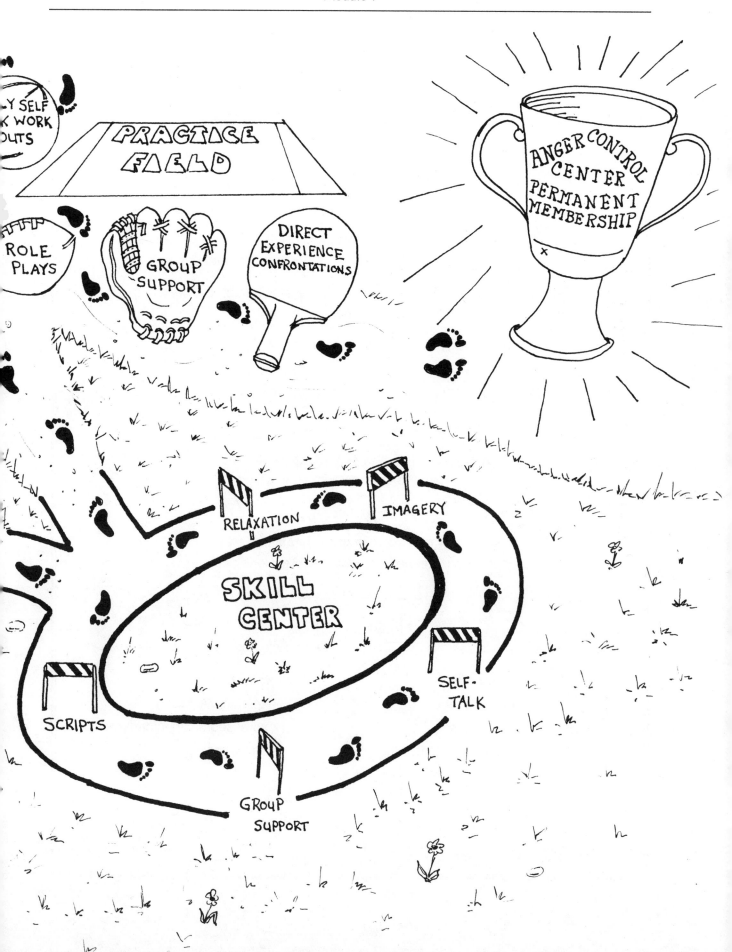

ANGER-MANAGEMENT SKILLS TRAINING
SOME DEFINITIONS

ANGER is a combination of discomfort, tenseness, resentment, and frustration.

ANGER is an IMMOBILIZING reaction,
experienced when our expectations are not met.

ANGER takes the form of rage, hostility, striking out at others,
or even the "silent treatment."

ANGER is NOT simple annoyance, irritation, disappointment.

ANGER is a choice, as well as a habit!
Like all emotions, it is the result of thinking!

ANGER-MANAGEMENT TRAINING IS NOT
trying to do away with feelings;

rather

ANGER-MANAGEMENT TRAINING IS
learning to increase appropriate expressions of anger.

ANGER CONTROL
means keeping expressions of anger at a manageable and nondestructive level.

Instead of:	Rather:
expressed rage	expressed irritation
verbal abuse	expressed disappointment
attacking or withdrawing	negotiating

UNCONTROLLED ANGER SEQUENCE

1. TRIGGERS:

- Anger Button Gets Pushed

⟱➡ ANGER REACTION OCCURS

2. THOUGHTS:

- Appraisals (our interpretations)
- Attributions (causes, blame assigned)
- Self-talk (what we say to ourselves)

⟱➡ INFLUENCE FEELINGS

3. FEELINGS:

- Threatened, Out of Control, Hurt
- Tension, Agitation, Turmoil

⟱➡ INTENSIFY ANGER REACTION

4. BEHAVIORS:

- Withdraw ⟵――――――➡ Attack

**⟱➡ INFLUENCE REACTION
AND CONSEQUENCES**

5. CONSEQUENCES:

- Negative Consequences

⟱➡ ESCALATE ANGER REACTION

UNCONTROLLED ANGER SEQUENCE
Discussion Outline

1. TRIGGERS:

SOMETHING HAPPENS, like you get criticized, and YOU GET ANGRY.

What are some things that push your button?

What causes you to get upset? To lose it?

(For example, bossing, yelling, "jumping on your back" when you haven't done anything, getting rejected.)

What are some things you've observed that make others mad?

2. THOUGHTS:

WE EVALUATE when our buttons get pushed; we THINK certain things, like "What a jerk!" or "How could I be so stupid!" or "He shouldn't act like that!" or "I can't take it anymore!"

THESE THOUGHTS ARE TRIGGERED BY OUR ATTITUDES, OUR BELIEFS, OUR BIASES!

What thoughts or ideas usually come to your mind when the things we identified happen to you?

What are some things we usually tell ourselves in our self-talk (e.g., "I'm going to show him!" or "_____!")?

3. FEELINGS:

OUR THINKING PRODUCES FEELINGS!

WE FEEL THE WAY WE THINK!

So, how do you usually feel in these situations we identified?

Emotionally?

(For example, anger is a secondary feeling that is aroused by other feelings, such as hurt and frustration.)

Physically?

(For example, what happens in parts of your body when you get really upset emotionally?)

4. BEHAVIORS:

UPSET FEELINGS GENERATE ACTIONS!

What do you do? How do you usually respond behaviorally?

5. CONSEQUENCES:

NEGATIVE BEHAVIORS USUALLY RESULT IN NEGATIVE CONSEQUENCES.

What are some consequences you often experience for getting out of control?

MAJOR THEMES

People express emotional upsets or problems in lots of ways:

- Some get depressed
  - Some get furious, angry
    - Some worry all the time—may get ulcers
      - Some feel worthless, inferior
        - Some have nervous breakdowns
          - Some consider or threaten suicide
            - Some use or abuse drugs
              - Some don't try, quit, and fail

Human beings have the unique capacity to think and reason;
therefore, we can change how we feel.

We feel the way we think..
Thinking produces **feelings**,
feelings generate actions or **behaviors**.

It's the way we think, our point of view!

It's our thinking, our ideas, our beliefs about something
(not the thing or event itself)
that cause us to feel upset.

So, nothing or nobody can make us feel angry, depressed, guilty,
worthless, like a failure, stupid, or whatever!

We create our own emotional upsets,
distresses, depression, anger—
by how we think!—our attitude!—our beliefs!—our biases!

This means we can change the way we feel
by changing our unrealistic thinking habits! Sounds easy!
But it takes effort, new skills, lots of practice!

———————

That's why we're here!
Problems become an opportunity for change

Change can occur—through effort, practicing new skills,
providing each other with feedback and support.

TODAY...

"I discovered that I..."

"I relearned that I..."

"I worried that I..."

"I'm concerned that I..."

"I'm pleased that I..."

"I wish that I..."

SCORING THE POMS*

Add up your points for items in each category:

1. Tension/Anxiety: (Ten) Add values you entered for: Enter Totals Here:

2___10___16___20___26___27___34___41___ = _____

Subtract score for #22___   _____

Total: _____ + 4   = _____

2. Depression: (Dep) Add values you entered for:

5___9___14___18___21___23___32___35___

36___44___45___48___58___61___62___   = _____

3. Anger: (Ang) Add values you entered for:

3___12___17___24___31___33___

39___42___47___52___53___57___   = _____

4. Vigor: (Vig) Add values you entered for:

7___15___19___38___51___56___60___63___   = _____

5. Fatigue: (Fat) Add values you entered for:

4___11___29___40___46___49___65___   = _____

6. Confusion/Uncertainty: (Con) Add values you entered for:

8___28___37___50___59___64___ =   _____

Subtract score for #54___   _____

Total: _____ + 4   = _____

- **Now, plot your scores on the POMS Profile Sheet:**
  1. Enter your total for each of the six scales in the RAW SCORE row at the bottom of the page.
  2. Circle the number in the corresponding column above each raw score; graph a line between scores.
  3. There is a corresponding T (or standard) score in the left/right columns for each of your raw scores.
     Your plotted and T scores tell you how you compare with the norms—whether you're above or below the 50% line—and which of these mood states is a problem for you.
- **In each case, the higher your score, the greater your anxiety, depression, anger, etc.**

*Scoring the POMS was developed by the author for use with the POMS test, which is copyrighted and can be obtained from the Educational and Industrial Testing Service (see page 156).

Getting to Know Your Anger Sequence

I. Background

Brief Description of the Module

This module reviews the anger sequence: Triggers, Thoughts, Feelings, Behaviors, and Consequences (TTFBC). It is designed to enhance self-exploration of a personal anger sequence and comparison with others' responses in the group. The central purpose is to engage and motivate students to:

1. identify their own external and internal anger triggers and their typical thoughts, feelings, behaviors, and consequences in response to these triggers; and

2. contemplate change and identify personal motivators for change.

Learning Objectives

Students will:

1. Identify five aspects of their own anger response sequence: TTFBC.

2. Know more about how they respond to distress or anger.

3. Identify motivators for contemplating alternative anger expressions.

Training Level

(X indicates those that apply to this module)

_X_ Skills Assessment (pre)   _X_ Skills Acquisition
___ Skills Assessment (post)   ___ Skills Application
_X_ Skills Monitoring/Check-Backs

Leader Strategies

In addition to encouraging and continuing to foster the development of a positive peer culture within the group, specific strategies the leader will be expected to use in this module are:

_X_ Instruction	___ Game
_X_ Modeling	___ Questionnaire/Scale
_X_ Group Discussion	___ Group Exercise
___ Group Practice	___ Role Play
_X_ Indiv/Dyad Practice	___ Real-Life Assignment
_X_ Homework	___ Other: _____

Attachments

1. The Uncontrolled Anger Sequence (cartoon version) (page 72).

2. My Typical Anger Triggers & Troublemakers (page 73).

3. Your Personal Anger Response Sequence: Discussion Outline (page 74).

4. Your Personal Anger Sequence form (page 76).

5. How I respond when I'm angry (Withdraw...Attack) (page 77).

6. How I respond when someone gets angry at me (Withdraw...Attack) (page 77).

Leader Preparations

Materials needed and things to do ahead of time include:

1. Handouts/teacher guides

   a. Discussion results of groups' TTFBC from Module 1

   b. Your Personal Anger Response Sequence Discussion Outline

   c. Your Personal Anger Sequence form

   d. My Typical Anger Triggers & Troublemakers

   e. 3x5 index cards, 10-15 for each student

   f. Major Themes (from Module 1)

2. Posters, overheads to make (or handouts)

   a. Anger-Management Trip Map (from Module 1)

   b. The Uncontrolled Anger Sequence (cartoon version)

   c. How I respond when I'm angry (Withdraw...Attack)

3. Review Monitoring/check-back activities from Module 1.

    a. Review notes about students to refresh your memory.

    b. Plan to repeat the Mood Diary ratings (see Getting Started, Welcome to Anger Management for Youth instructions, and attachment).

4. Review your self-analysis notes from the last session.

    a. Plan to repeat liberally the strengths you identified.

    b. Focus on the growth objectives you listed, but not so strenuously that you forget your strengths.

5. Set up equipment for video taping session.

Implementation Guidelines

Part I: Motivational Preparation
Provide the "what, how, and why" (i.e., motivators, persuasive strategies).

See Uncontrolled Anger Sequence (cartoon version). use to briefly review the prior session's activities and insights in order to capture attention and recall of TTFBC.

Post the student-generated list of TTFBC results from the Module 1 discussion. Give each student a typed copy of this list. Ask students to use this list to stimulate their thinking as they take the next step: *personalizing the sequence for themselves.*

Refer to the posted results from the POMS and from the Mood Diary results. Link those results to today's work.

At the end of our last session, I asked you to think about a situation when you got very angry, to think about what triggered the anger, what thoughts this provoked, how this influenced your feelings, how your feelings then influenced your behavior, and what consequences resulted. What are some situations that came to your mind? Facilitate brief reports.

Make a transition into the objectives for this module. Have students look at the Anger-Management Trip Map in their notebook so that they can visualize where they are going and what they will be doing.

Part II: Learning Activities/Process Guidelines

1. Individual Insight Work: the Personal Anger Response Sequence Exercise.

See Your Personal Anger Response Sequence Discussion Outline. Implement that discussion now. Give each student a Personal Anger Sequence form and 10-15 3x5 index cards.

Talk the group through each step, having individuals report results on their papers. Model the same behavior you are asking of the students.

Alternative exercise

If students have difficulty filling out the index cards with triggers, it may be useful to start first with the questionnaire form: My Typical Anger Triggers & Troublemakers.

If you use this form:

> Pass out a copy to each student and ask them to quickly check the situations—*Yes, Maybe, No.*

> Survey the group for each item; i.e., ask for a show of hands and record how many "yes" answers there are for each item. Ask a volunteer to record these results on the flip chart or on an overhead. This will give you and the group an opportunity to discover which triggers and troublemakers are most common for people in the group.

> Follow with a discussion of examples of specific situations for the more common "triggers."

> Next, have students complete the index cards for step 1 in Your Personal Anger Sequence.

2. Dyad work

Have students share their work in pairs (e.g., with person sitting next to them or with someone they haven't worked with yet).

Instruct students to interview each other to:

- understand and clarify the person's anger response sequence to one of their troublesome triggers and troublemakers; and

- compile a list of triggers and troublemakers they both listed in their index cards.

3. Group Discussion

Bring the group back together and ask students to:

- Identify one of their troublemakers. Either record on flip chart list from Module 1 or start a new list.

- Identify the shared triggers and troublemakers in the group; ask a group member to record these on the flip chart.

Now, let's find out how each of you usually responds when you get angry. (Use the Withdraw...Attack scale handout.)

On a scale of 1 to 10, with Withdraw being a 1 and Attack a 10, think about how you usually respond to a specific trigger you identified. Pick the trigger and then pick a number between 1 and 10, circling it in the first box. Now how about your response to one of your troublemakers? Rate it. Next, consider how you respond when someone blows up at you! Circle a number between 1 and 10 in that box.

O.K., let's have reports. The goal here is to find out where everyone is on the continuum so we know what we're dealing with. I'll start and admit that I often tend to _____, so I gave myself a "_____" for that one.

Go around the circle to collect numbers from group members. List the numbers students gave themselves in two columns. The first column is how they respond when angry, and the second is for how they respond when someone blows up at them. Use the flip chart to record the results. Be sure to keep this information, study it, and use it for future comparisons of progress.

4. Contemplating Change—Transition to Learning Alternative Responses

Turn to a clean page on the flip chart and lead the group discussion into:

What would you like to have happen instead?

and

What would motivate you to start learning some new patterns of responding to anger that would "save face" and be less harmful to yourself and others?

Use these discussion results to introduce the next step on the posted Anger-Management Trip Map: some strategies and techniques that will be learned together, starting with the activities in Module 3.

Part III: Wrapping It Up

1. Summarize, Promote Insight, Personalize

Give positive feedback for a great day and good work. Personalize this with specific observations you made. Point out and positively reinforce the things group members said they would like to do differently, or those things that would motivate them to start learning new patterns of behavior in response to anger.

Go around the circle and ask students to report one thing they learned or relearned today.

Have students put the index cards in their notebooks.

Ask students to turn in their anger-response ratings or to put the date on them and keep them in their notebook.

2. Promote "Taking It Away!"

Homework, Transfer activities/assignments

Have students look at the Major Themes handout from Module 1 and ask them to select one theme to repeat several times as "self-talk" between today and the next session.

Part IV: Monitoring/Check-Back Activities

The group generated some important material during this session. Take time to review the lists of common triggers and troublemakers. Type a list and make copies for each student or prepare a poster of this information and post it in the room for review during the next session.

Type the list of things the students said would motivate them to start learning new patterns of behavior. Study this list carefully so that you can recall these points in the next group session.

Other things to remember are:

_____

_____

_____

_____

_____

_____

_____

_____

Guided Self-Analysis

Review the videotape of your group session.

Using the lists of Leader Competencies from Chapter 1, complete the following:

Leader Competencies for Fostering the Group-Support System

Examples of strengths in fostering group support I observed were:

1. _____

2. _____

3. _____

4. _____

5. _____

A growth objective to work on next time is:

_____

_____

Leader Competencies for Fostering the Skills-Training Component

Examples of strengths in skills training I observed were:

1. _____

2. _____

3. _____

4. _____

5. _____

A growth objective to work on next time is:

_____

_____

I am particularly proud of:

_____

_____

UNCONTROLLED ANGER SEQUENCE

1. TRIGGERS:

SOMETHING UNPLEASANT

HAPPENS

2. THOUGHTS

WE EVALUATE—

WE THINK TO OURSELVES

3. FEELINGS

THEN WE FEEL

THE WAY WE THINK!

4. BEHAVIORS

WE ACT OUT

OUR FEELINGS!

5. CONSEQUENCES

NEGATIVE CONSEQUENCES

ESCALATE OUR ANGER!

MY TYPICAL ANGER
TRIGGERS & TROUBLEMAKERS*

I GET ANGRY WHEN:	YES	MAYBE	NO
1. Someone lets me down.	___	___	___
2. People are unfair.	___	___	___
3. Something blocks my plans.	___	___	___
4. Someone embarrasses me.	___	___	___
5. I am delayed, held up.	___	___	___
6. I have to take orders from someone.	___	___	___
7. I have to work with incompetent people.	___	___	___
8. I do something stupid!	___	___	___
9. I don't get credit for what I've done.	___	___	___
10. Someone puts me down.	___	___	___
11. _____ (other)	___	___	___
12. _____ (other)	___	___	___

*Adapted from Seigel, J.M. (1986). The multidimensional anger inventory. *Journal of Personality & Social Psychology, 51*, p. 200. Copyright © 1986 by the American Psychological Association. Adapted by permission.

YOUR PERSONAL ANGER RESPONSE SEQUENCE

Discussion Outline

1. TRIGGERS:

Triggers set us off! But how we think, feel, and act once one of our buttons is pushed is learned. *Some of the ways we respond are* unhealthy. *The good news is that because these ways were* learned, *we can* unlearn *our unhealthy responses and* learn *new, healthy responses.*

But first, what are triggers? Here are some new terms for you to think about.

- *Triggers can be* external *or* internal.

- *External triggers are events or things that happen to you, that are in your environment.*

- *Internal triggers occur inside yourself as thoughts, feelings, or sensations.*

Jot down on your index cards all the external and internal triggers you can think of—one per card—including those things you've learned to react to with anger, those things that push your Anger Button—the big RED one in the middle of your chest. (Work at the same task to model the behavior. Monitor time.)

Now arrange your cards in a hierarchy—from MOST to LEAST upsetting triggers.

Your most upsetting triggers are your troublemakers! These can be both external *and* internal.

Continue the exercise by having each student select two to three of their top troublemakers. Ask them to list these on their Personal Anger Sequence forms.

2. THOUGHTS:

As I ask you questions, I want you to write down your answer in the "THOUGHTS" section. Here goes:

What do you typically say to yourself when each of these troublemakers gets to you? What is your attitude, your thinking? Write down as many as you think of. Look over the list we generated yesterday—which apply to you?

Why is this situation so awful, terrible, for you? What are your beliefs that are being violated by these troublemakers? Write them down, please.

And how do you escalate the situation by your thinking? Your self-talk? Write down what you say to yourself.

3. FEELINGS

Refer to the list that students produced in the last session. Ask them:
How do you typically feel in each situation you picked—one of the feelings we identified during our last session? Or maybe another one we didn't identify?

You may feel differently in response to each troublemaker you selected. Write down your feelings on your form—as many as you can identify.

4. BEHAVIORS

And what is your typical response: verbal or physical? Withdraw vs. Attack? Where are you on the continuum? How would I know? What could I observe about you? Write down how you would typically behave.

5. CONSEQUENCES

What consequences do you typically experience? What are all the things that usually happen to you after you behave as you described above?

ANGER MANAGEMENT FOR YOUTH

YOUR PERSONAL ANGER SEQUENCE

1. TRIGGERS:

2. THOUGHTS:

3. FEELINGS:

4. BEHAVIORS:

5. CONSEQUENCES:

HOW I RESPOND WHEN I'M ANGRY

WITHDRAW   *ATTACK*

1..2..3..4..5..6..7..8..9..10

HOW I RESPOND WHEN SOMEONE GETS ANGRY AT ME

WITHDRAW   *ATTACK*

1..2..3..4..5..6..7..8..9..10

Taking Control of Your Anger Responses—I

I. Background

Brief Description of the Module

This module is the first in a series to train for anger control. It is designed to personalize the student's personal triggers and troublemakers: anger-provoking external situations (events) and internal triggers (thoughts, emotions, sensations). More important, this module focuses on acquiring specific skills: self-talk, relaxation, guided imagery. These techniques are designed for use in two (of four) anger-control stages:

Stage 1. Inoculations for before anger buttons are pushed, and

Stage 2. Control strategies to use when the anger response is first triggered.

This module is the first in the skills building component of *Anger Management for Youth*. Whereas Modules 1 and 2 comprised primarily self-assessment and motivating students to consider behavior change, this module gets down to the business of learning new, helpful ways of responding to anger triggers and troublemakers.

Skills building for Stages 3 and 4 of the anger-control strategies (techniques for coping during and after being provoked to anger) are taught and practiced in Module 4 (Chapter 6).

Learning Objectives

During and after the learning activities presented in this module, students will:

1. Commit to learning specific anger-control responses for

    a. getting "inoculated" against uncontrolled anger and

    b. keeping their "cool" when first triggered or provoked to anger.

2. Decide on one trigger or troublemaker they will use for practicing the targeted anger-management skills.

3. Select appropriate self-talk statements to rehearse in relation to their troublemakers for the "before" and "when triggered" anger stages.

4. Practice applying relaxation techniques and imagery for "keeping your cool."

5. Practice appropriate verbal and nonverbal responses to control anger.

Training Level

(X indicates those that apply to this module)

_X_ Skills Assessment   _X_ Skills Acquisition
_X_ Skills Application   _X_ Skills Monitoring/Check-Backs

Leader Strategies

In addition to encouraging and fostering a culture of caring within the group, specific strategies the leader is expected to use in this module are:

_X_ Instruction   ___ Game

_X_ Modeling   _X_ Questionnaire/Scale

_X_ Group Discussion   _X_ Group Exercise

_X_ Group Practice   _X_ Role Play

_X_ Indiv/Dyad Practice   _X_ Real-Life Assignment

_X_ Homework   ___ Other: _____

Attachments

1. Summary—Insights (page 91)

2. Some Faces of Harmful Anger Expressions (page 92)

3. Anger Sequence (page 93)

4. Why You Choose Anger: 12 Typical Motives (page 94)

5. Self-talk Examples to Rehearse for Controlling Anger (page 95)

6. Guided Imagery for Anger and Mood Control (page 96)

Leader Preparations

Materials needed and things to do ahead of time include:

1. Handouts/Teacher Guides

a. Summary—Insights, to review sessions 1 and 2. Post a large copy of this and also make a copy for each student's binder.

b. Anger Sequence (a copy for each student).

c. Some Faces of Harmful Anger Expressions (a copy for each student).

d. Why You Choose Anger: 12 Typical Motives (a copy for each student).

e. Self-talk Examples to Rehearse for Controlling Anger (a copy for each student).

f. Guided Imagery for Anger and Mood Control. Rehearse this before the group session. Record your voice and play back the recording to make sure you sound "soothing" and not nervous or uncomfortable.

2. Posters, Overheads to Make (or Handouts)

a. Post a large copy of Faces of Harmful Anger Expressions in the group room.

b. Anger-Management Trip Map poster from Module 1—"Skill Center is the focus now."

c. Poster of list of common triggers and troublemakers generated during the last session. Also type a copy for each student.

3. Review Monitoring and Check-Back Notes from Previous Session

a. Make notes of how and when to incorporate.

b. Review your notes for important student information to recall.

4. Set up equipment for video taping session.

Implementation Guidelines

Part I: Motivational Preparation

Recall: The purpose of this module is to motivate the students by providing the "what, how, and why" and by using persuasive communication and social influence strategies to get the students involved. Generally, this means you must

• Reveal the objectives in an interesting manner.

• Promote the perceived purpose.

• Describe strategies as appealing and valuable.

1. Inspire, Motivate

In your own words, genuinely and convincingly emphasize that today they're going to be exposed to some real "treasures"— strategies that are the best available and that have proven to be effective. Personalize this message by relating briefly how these techniques have worked for you. Pick something and relate your story in a way that helps students to identify easily with you.

Lay the foundation and get students to "buy-in" and commit to skills by appealing to one or more powerful motivators:

- personal gain
- convenience
- pleasure
- love and acceptance
- imitation
- security
- prestige
- new experience
- desire to avoid fear or embarrassment

2. Reveal Objectives

Use the Summary—Insights poster to summarize sessions 1 and 2 and to make your points.

Hand out copies of Summary—Insights and have students put it in their three-ring binder. Engage the group in brief self-disclosures of personal experiences with these insights. This also may be an opportune time to conduct the follow-up monitoring or to share your observations of students' progress from the previous group session.

Refer to the Anger-Management Trip Map poster. Point out that starting today, students will work in the "Skill Center."

Our objective is to learn about and practice managing anger and conflicts with "sophistication."

Knowing what triggers our anger and what our troublemakers are isn't enough. But, it is an important first step.

Old habits die hard. But, stubborn human nature and old ways can be changed. Both are susceptible to change efforts and lots of practice.

3. Promote Perceived Purposes

To prevent harmful consequences to ourselves and others that almost always occur as a result of uncontrolled anger expressions. (Refer to the poster, Some Faces of Harmful Anger Expressions, to illustrate your point.)

To promote getting along better with friends, family, and future loved ones.

Remember: people have a hard time loving aggressive, abusive bullies.

4. How Do We Change?

By "buying-into" changing. By deciding we need to and want to change. By dropping the denial and defensiveness and accepting personal responsibility.

By practice, practice, practice of new behaviors to become competent, skilled, and sophisticated.

By contracting for support and for feedback on skills.

By monitoring and tracking skill development and goal achievement.

Most important, by experiencing the rewards of new behaviors in personal relationships with friends, with teachers, with family, and others.

By setting goals for changing specific behaviors and attitudes.

By starting today! By starting with easy problems so that success is guaranteed. If we try to tackle our worst troublemakers first, we're more likely to fail and then think "it won't work." But the strategies we're going to learn do work.

Describe strategies.

These strategies have worked successfully, for example, with persons having both mild and chronic anger problems (For example, teens, adults, police officers, persons who got into trouble with the law, and so forth).

These coping strategies include:

- *"Inoculations"—self-talk rehearsals*

- *Relaxation techniques*

- *Scripts to use in difficult situations*

- *Problem-solving skills for negotiation and conflict resolution*

Today the targeted skills are the inoculations and relaxation techniques

Part II: Learning Activities/Process Guidelines

A reminder of your leadership role:

- Provide relevant information and examples.
- Model the skills in your own behavior.
- Provide appropriate practice for everyone.
- Provide for large "doses" of group support.

1. Self-Exploration (Imagery) Individual Exercise

I'd like each of you to close your eyes and think of a situation where you really got angry. Pretend you're "running a movie" of the event. Picture the scene and the people there. (pause)

Now, relive the experience and identify: what set you off? what triggered your anger? (pause)

Next, why do you think you got angry? What were you thinking at the time? (pause)

What expectations did you have that weren't met? Like, what didn't you get that you wanted or thought you had a right to have? (pause)

Hand out copies of the Anger Sequence form (page 93).

O.K. Now I want you to write down on the Anger Sequence handout the trigger, your thoughts, and your feelings. Then, recall how you behaved. What did you say? What did you do? Write that down.

Follow this written work by going around the circle and having each person:

a. report particular aspects of the provoking situation. (What was the situation? What particulars led to "losing your cool"?).

b. report their thoughts and unmet expectations.

Introduce the idea of gaining insights into reasons for using anger:

"Getting a grip" and "lengthening our fuses" will start when we gain some insight. Here are some of the psychological motives we typically use for keeping our fuse as short as it is:

Hand out Why You Choose Anger: 12 Typical Motives. Ask each student to look over the list and place a check mark next to all the reasons they used anger in the anger situation they just relived.

Go around the circle and encourage students to report the insights they gained.

If necessary, model by going first.

Summarize the group discussion of the insights they gained; suggest that the feelings of anger they experienced were influenced by the things they said to themselves.

Transition: The basic idea of anger management is that anger starts, is maintained, and is "fueled" by the self-statements we make in anger-provoking situations. So, a basic way of gaining control is to change what we're saying to ourselves—changing our anger-producing self-statements to anger-controlling ones. Let's work on that now.

2. Self-Talk Inoculations: A Coping Strategy

Introduce this exercise. For example,

Anger can be eliminated. It will require a lot of new thinking, and it can be done only one moment at a time.

We can "inoculate" ourselves against anger.

When confronted with people or events that provoke us to choose anger, we can become aware of what we are telling ourselves. We can work out a new script that will create new feelings and more constructive, lovable behavior.

Pass out the handout Self-Talk Examples to Rehearse.

Have students focus on the self-talk used for each of the first two stages:

1. Preparing for anger triggers and

2. When confronted, when my button is pushed.

Explain that this exercise will be covered both today and in the next group session. The students will target Stages 1 and 2 today, then Stages 3 and 4 next time.

Have students work in groups of two or three.

Ask them to select examples for the "before" and "when confronted" stages that they could see themselves using.

Ask them also to record on a sheet of paper additional statements that they would use—ones that achieve the same purposes.

When each small group is finished, reconvene the large group and have students report their results to the total group.

Finally, compare the new scripts generated with the Self-Talk Examples handout to see:

1. if their additions are communicating the same central message and are in the same spirit;

2. which ones the group votes on to add to the handout. (Note: When you have your group generate ideas like this, be sure to follow-up by having the list retyped to reflect their additions and then post it or give everyone a copy for their notebooks.)

- Ask each person to select two statements for each stage, ones that they will commit to using with one of the specific triggers they identified. Next, go around the circle and have everyone report his or her choices.

  Record the most favored choices on the flip chart and report these back to the group as a way of summarizing.

  Note: Tell the students that these choices are important for everyone to remember, and to use as a kind of "group culture." These are reinforcing statements that all can subscribe to.

3. Coping With Anger—A Scripting Strategy

Applying Self-Talk to Specific Triggers and Troublemakers

Introduction: *One way of learning to control anger is to develop a new script. We've talked about our personal triggers and troublemakers. I've posted the most common ones we identified last session (refer to poster).*

Now we're going to start working on controlling ourselves when triggered and in danger of losing control.

Have group members recall the trigger or troublemaker they visualized earlier. However, if the one they chose is not a relatively simple situation, then have them select one simple trigger from the list of common triggers and troublemakers generated last session (refer to the poster or hand out a copy for each student).

Ask students what "faces" of harmful anger expressions they experience in their chosen trigger situation (see Some Faces of Harmful Anger Expressions handout). Go around the circle and encourage self-disclosure.

Finally, ask students what the results usually have been for "losing their cool" in their situation. For example:

- looking foolish
- making the situation worse
- getting grounded, suspended
- hurting someone
- regretting behavior

- losing a chance or an opportunity

Again, encourage group sharing and have one of the group members record their statements on the flip chart.

4. Relaxation—A Coping Strategy for Keeping Your Cool under Fire The Quieting Response (QR)

- Instruct and demonstrate.

  Show students how to take in a deep abdominal breath (the abdomen should expand and not just the chest), hold it, then slowly let it out to the count of 10 (about 1 second per count).

- Practice together. Coach as follows:

Take in a deep breath. Push out your abdomen with it and hold it. Now slowly let it out to the count of 10:
1 . . . 2 . . . 3 . . . 4 . . . 5 . . . 6 . . . 7 . . . 8 . . . 9 . . . 10

Good job! Now lean forward, shake yourself lose of body tensions, and let's practice it again.

(Repeat the above without rushing the count.)

The QR is especially important for handling triggers and troublemakers—to keep you from responding impulsively and "losing your cool." I often use it in the car if I'm getting uptight and angry about the traffic. I use it before I go on stage if I have to make a speech. And I use it every time I notice that my shoulders are getting tense and I'm feeling stressed.

Guided Imagery

Now, implement the guided imagery exercise (see page 96) to demonstrate how this strategy can work to foster a positive mood and a sense of well-being.

Part III: Wrapping It Up

1. Summarize, Promote Insight, Personalize

A reminder: Guide the group through closure!

- Ask some of the group to summarize major points.

- Check for comprehension.

- Check for personalization. Use the Today...I Discovered... poster.

- Model the skills in your own behavior.

Reinforce by sharing specifics you observed in skill development for each individual and in the group's work and peer support.

2. Promote "Taking It Away!"

Some reminders of how to promote "taking it away":

- Have students apply skills to "easy" situations first to set up no-loss situations and promote success. Have each student report to the group the self-talk they will apply in a specific, relatively uncomplicated situation between now and the next group, and when they plan to use and practice the QR.

  Monitor to make sure the situations are simple ones. And record the students' choices so that you can follow-up next session.

- Inspire:

Successful situations motivate and reinforce skill development and confidence!

- For discouraged, negative, "it-won't-work" types, point out evidence that it might work and the gains to the student if it does.

- Point out things to be proud of now, despite the difficulties. Focus on the present source of difficulty.

- Reinforce:

Learning new behaviors takes practice and more practice. More productive ways to behave bring desired rewards.

Model, model, model the skills in your own behavior.

Part IV: Monitoring/Check-Back Activities

Tell the students:

On the top of the next session's agenda will be "Check-In" reports of our success stories in using the QR and in using self-talk inoculations.

Student commitments to remember are:

Student's Name   Commitments Made

_____

_____

_____

_____

_____

_____

_____

_____

_____

_____

_____

_____

• See also the Appendix for sample TTFBC check-back tools to use (page 142).

Guided Self-Analysis

Review the videotape of your group session.

Using the lists of Leader Competencies from Chapter 1, complete the following:

Leader Competencies for Fostering the Group-Support System

Examples of strengths in fostering group support I observed were:

1. _____
2. _____
3. _____
4. _____
5. _____

A growth objective to work on next time is:

_____

_____

Leader Competencies for Fostering the Skills-Training Component

Examples of strengths in skills training I observed were:

1. _____
2. _____
3. _____
4. _____
5. _____

A growth objective to work on next time is:

_____

_____

I am particularly proud of:

_____

_____

SUMMARY—INSIGHTS

1. Upsetting feelings (depression, anger, worry, helplessness, etc.) are caused by our upsetting ideas, by our thoughts!

2. We stay angry, depressed, stressed, etc., because we keep telling ourselves upsetting ideas over and over (what's awful, what shouldn't be, what's stupid, etc.). We can make ourselves more angry or depressed because we also tend to exaggerate the upsetting ideas with each telling.

3. We can stay angry, depressed, and anxious if we like, or we can change the way we think. We can challenge our mental list of "Awfuls and Terribles."

4. Just knowing we need to change is not enough—old habits remain as habits when they are left alone!

5. To change takes effort, learning new skills, and lots of practice! Remember, our existing habits also came from lots of practice too. So, it's going to take lots of practice to learn new habits!

6. With conscious effort and lots of practice, the likelihood is that we won't get as upset, as often, as long as we do now.

SOME FACES OF HARMFUL ANGER EXPRESSIONS*

PHYSICAL VIOLENCE   Hitting, kicking, and slamming objects or people. Carried to extremes, this leads to assaults and other crimes of violence. These occur when anger is out of control.

VERBAL ABUSE   Ridicule, insults, name-calling, yelling, and shouting at loved ones, friends, or others.

Also, phrases like "kill her/him!" "clobber them," or "destroy 'em!" may seem like O.K. expressions, but they incite anger and violence and can make them acceptable even in friendly competition.

TEMPER TANTRUMS   A common expression of anger that is selfish indulgence. It can lead to verbal or physical abuse of others.

SARCASM and the SILENT TREATMENT   Like ridicule and put-downs, these anger expressions can be just as hurtful as physical violence.

BLAMING   Saying things like "you really aggravate me!" or "you make me so mad!" Here you're blaming someone else for your own anger.

A SOBERING NOTE   Uncontrolled anger is not normal!

The philosophy that advocates getting in touch with your anger and "letting it all hang out" can be potentially dangerous to yourself and others.

Popularized anger and violence (e.g., in television, movies, books) which portrays them as normal undermines both individuals like you and me and our society as well.

*Adapted from Dyer, W. (1977). Farewell to Anger, in *Your Erroneous Zones*. NY: Avon Books.

ANGER SEQUENCE

1. TRIGGERS:

2. THOUGHTS:

3. FEELINGS:

4. BEHAVIORS:

5. CONSEQUENCES:

WHY YOU CHOOSE ANGER: 12 TYPICAL MOTIVES
You can haul out the old anger and throw a little tantrum when you want:

1. To manipulate those who are afraid of you—typically younger, smaller folks.

2. A handy excuse. ("I couldn't help it.")

3. To get your way. (Others would rather give in to you than put up with your anger.)

4. To avoid intimacy or sharing yourself affectionately (if you are afraid of this).

5. To break down communication when you feel threatened by someone else's competence.

6. To get attention, to be important and powerful.

7. To avoid hard, straight thinking.

8. To excuse poor performance or losing.

9. To direct responsibility to someone else instead of taking charge of yourself.

10. To feel sorry for yourself (self-pity).

11. To manipulate others with guilt.

12. To take the heat off yourself—to avoid working on self-improvement.

WARNING: *Violence is destructive to yourself and others!*

SELF-TALK EXAMPLES TO REHEARSE FOR CONTROLLING ANGER
Stages 1 and 2

(Adapted from Novaco, 1975)

Preparing for "anger triggers"—things that "push my button"

This is going to be upsetting, but I can handle it.

This doesn't have to be a catastrophe.

Stop! Figure out what I have to do...work out a plan.

I can manage this. I know how to control my anger.

I'll know what to do if I find myself getting upset...

  relax, take a deep breath, remember my plan.

Don't overreact. Don't blow this out of proportion.

This could be a sticky situation, but I believe in myself.

Time for the QR. Feel comfortable, relaxed, at ease.

Easy does it. Remember to keep my sense of humor.

Easy does it. Remember my lines.

When confronted, when my "button is pushed"

Stop! Stay calm. Think! Don't jump to conclusions.

Do the QR, or count to 10.

Don't blow things out of proportion.

So it hurts! There's no use stretching it into an

  awful, dreadful, terrible situation.

As long as I keep my cool, I'm in control.

Don't get bent out of shape. Stick with the plan.

I don't need to prove myself. I know I am O.K.

There is no point in getting out of control.

Don't make more of this than I have to.

Look for the positives. Don't assume the worst.

If I start to get mad, I'll just be banging my head

  against the wall. So I might as well just relax.

There is no need to doubt myself. I can handle this!

I'm on top of the situation, and it's under control.

GUIDED IMAGERY FOR ANGER AND MOOD CONTROL

Close your eyes and focus your attention on your breath. As you breathe in...and out...gently through your nose or mouth, allow yourself to become more and more relaxed. As you gently breathe in...and...out, your feet become relaxed (pause)...your legs become relaxed (pause)...your abdomen becomes relaxed (pause)...your back and shoulders become relaxed (pause)...your arms and hands become limp and relaxed. And as you continue to breathe in...and...out, gently and quietly, your head becomes relaxed...and your mind floats free, and you find yourself floating away from this room to a wonderful island...a place where you really like to be. It is a place where you feel really safe. It is a place in nature...you feel good about yourself here...you feel at peace. (Pause.) Enjoy being there! Enjoy the warmth of the sun...and breathe it into yourself...filling yourself with warmth and love. Breathe it in again.

Now, see yourself as absolutely at peace...as you want to be...with yourself...with a friend...with your family. See yourself doing and enjoying something you do well—whether it be sports...school...work...crafts... music...drawing...being a good listener...a good observer...being a good friend. Just experience yourself as an absolute jewel...and enjoy yourself... enjoy the peace. Let any feelings of anger just melt away...see them oozing out of your pores and disappearing! Choose instead the warmth of the sun and the feeling of peace and well-being. Think positively about yourself and your growing ability to let go of anger and enjoy peace, quiet, and yourself as you want to be...for the next minute of silence, enjoy the warmth, love, and peace on your island.

(After a Minute) Now I'm going to call you back to this room. Bring the feeling of warmth and well-being with you. You can carry it with you throughout the rest of the day. I will count to three. (Pause.) 1...2...3. Open your eyes...and...welcome back. I'm glad you're here.

Taking Control of Your Anger Responses—II

I. Background

Brief Description of the Module

This module is the second in the series of training for anger control. It is designed to help the participants respond constructively in anger-provoking external situations (events) and internal triggers (thoughts, emotions, sensations). This module advances the previous one by focusing on additional skills: self-talk, coping with anger, and decision-making. These techniques are designed for use in Stages 3 and 4 of anger control:

Stage 3. Coping when already aroused and angry, and

Stage 4. Reflecting after the event, during "play-back."

This module continues the Skills Building component of *Anger Management for Youth*. It gets down to the business of learning new, helpful ways of responding when already angry and afterward, when thinking about the conflict.

Learning Objectives

During and after the learning activities presented in this module, students will:

1. Review the specific anger-control responses for

   Stage 1, getting "inoculated" against uncontrolled anger, and

   Stage 2, keeping their "cool" when first triggered or provoked to anger.

2. Commit to learning specific anger-control responses for

   Stage 3, coping when already angry or starting to "fume," and

   Stage 4, reflecting after the event when conflict is resolved or unresolved.

3. Select appropriate self-talk statements to rehearse in relation to a "troublemaker" for the "during" and "after" anger stages.

4. Learn and practice applying the C O P I N G model of anger-management strategies.

5. Define and practice the S T O M P model for impulse control in anger-provoking situations.

Training Level

(X indicates those that apply to this module)

_X_ Skills Assessment   _X_ Skills Acquisition
_X_ Skills Application   _X_ Skills Monitoring/Check-Backs

Leader Strategies

In addition to encouraging and fostering a culture of caring within the group, specific strategies the leader is expected to use in this module are:

_X_ Instruction   ___ Game

_X_ Modeling   _X_ Questionnaire/Scale

_X_ Group Discussion   _X_ Group Exercise

_X_ Group Practice   _X_ Role Play

_X_ Indiv/Dyad Practice   _X_ Real-Life Assignment

_X_ Homework   ___ Other: _____

Attachments

1. Self-Talk Examples to Rehearse for Controlling Anger—for Stages 3 and 4 (page 113).

2. C O P I N G With Anger: The Steps (page 114).

3. S T O M P—A Decision-Making Model (page 115).

Leader Preparations

Materials needed and things to do ahead of time include:

1. Handouts/Teacher Guides

   a. Guided Imagery for Anger and Mood Control—(from Module 3—teacher guide)

b. Self-Talk Examples to Rehearse for Controlling Anger—Stages 3 and 4 (a copy for each student)

c. C O P I N G with Anger: The Steps (a copy for each student)

d. S T O M P: A Decision-Making Model (a copy for each student)

2. Posters or Overheads to Make

a. Post in the room large copies of:

- Faces of Harmful Anger Expressions

- Anger-Management Trip Map

- Common Triggers and Troublemakers (use the list generated by the group in the last module)

b. Retype the list of Self-Talk Examples to Rehearse for Controlling Anger (for Stages 1 and 2) to include those examples the group voted to add and delete those they found "unusable." Make a copy for each student to replace the original version.

c. Post a large copy of the S T O M P handout in the room.

d. Write the words that form the acronym, S T O M P, on a 6-foot-long piece of butcher paper. Another option is to make separate squares for each word on pieces of construction paper; each square should be large enough for a student to stand on.

3. Review Monitoring and Check-Back Notes from Previous Session

a. Record on the flip chart each student's self-talk and QR commitments made for rehearsals during the week. Place this item on the posted agenda for the day.

b. Personalize—review your notes for important student information to recall and check back on progress. Make notes in the implementation plan section of this module for appropriate places to incorporate.

c. See also the Appendix for sample TTFBC check-back tools to use if desired.

4. Set up equipment for video taping session.

Implementation Guidelines

Part I: Motivational Preparation

Recall: The purpose is to motivate by providing the "what, how, and why," using persuasive communication and social influence strategies to maintain the students' involvement at this stage. Again, this means you

- Reveal the objectives in an interesting manner.

- Promote the perceived purpose.

- Describe the strategies as appealing and valuable.

1. Inspire, Motivate

Provide positive feedback for the fine work they started last session on building skills for anger control. Give concrete examples of what you observed that showed real growth in maturity and behavior change.

2. Reveal Objectives

Refer to the Anger-Management Trip Map poster. Point out:

We're going to do more work in the "Skill Center."

Our objective is to continue learning about and practicing managing anger and conflicts with "sophistication."

3. Reinforce Perceived Purposes

To prevent harmful consequences to ourselves and others that almost always occur as a result of uncontrolled anger expressions (for example, from physical and verbal abuse, assaults, fights, and so forth). Refer to the poster, Some Faces of Harmful Anger Expressions, to illustrate your point.

To promote getting along better with friends, family, and future loved ones.

Remember: People have a hard time loving aggressive, abusive bullies.

Reinforce how these behavior changes will undoubtedly reap valuable rewards for them personally and in their friendships; that is, a greater likelihood for:

- personal gain
- security
- pleasure
- love, acceptance
- less fear and embarrassment

4. Reinforce How We Change

By "buying-into" changing. By deciding we need to and want to. By dropping the denial and defensiveness and accepting personal responsibility.

By setting goals for changing specific behaviors and attitudes. By contracting for support, for feedback on skills.

By experiencing the rewards of new behaviors in personal relationships—with friends, with teachers, with family, etc.

By starting with easy problems so that we can learn the skills. Trying to tackle the big troublemakers first, before we really make the skills a part of us, does not work; we are more likely to fail and then think, "it won't work, this is stupid!" or worse, think, "I'm stupid, I can never get it."

By practice, practice, practice of new behaviors in order to become competent and sophisticated so that the skills become a natural part of us.

Most important, by monitoring and tracking our progress, our successes, our achievements along our Anger-Management Trip.

Last session we focused on what to do before and when triggered to respond with uncontrolled anger.

These coping strategies included self-talk "inoculations" and relaxation techniques.

Today, we're going to focus on strategies for coping when we already are angry, when we're "fuming." We also will focus on strategies for after the event, when we're on "play back" in our minds.

These target strategies include scripts to use in tight situations, coping and negotiating techniques, and a decision-making model.

Part II: Learning Activities/Process Guidelines

A reminder of your leadership role:

- Provide for large doses of group support.

- Provide for "check-backs" to monitor progress and to provide lots of positive feedback and encouragement.

- Provide relevant information and examples.

- Model the skills in your own behavior.

- Provide appropriate practice for everyone.

1. Check-Backs of Success Stories

Introduce, motivate.

Use "Check-In" procedure to get reports of success stories, of how it went in implementing their self-talk and QR commitments.

Hand out your retyped, revised version of Self-Talk Examples to Rehearse for Controlling Anger. Point out that this version includes their additions and deletions from their work last session.

Group shares.

Use the flip chart list of commitments that individuals made to use self-talk examples and the QR. Go around the circle and get reports of how it went. Model and coach the group in giving positive reinforcement for all attempts made in the desired direction.

Group supports, positively reinforces.

Provide a lot of positive feedback and little or no negative feedback. Provide a lot of invitations to get on board and few or no "guilt trips" for not doing so. For those who didn't keep their commitments, ask what it would take to give it a try some time today. Focus most on those who kept their commitments and provide for lots of positive reinforcement from the group. Model this in your own responses.

Group discusses, individuals gain insight.

> Invite group discussion of the insights gained from their own experiences or from one that someone else reported. Model by going first if necessary.

> Summarize the group discussion of the insights gained. Actively point out the skills used and provide insights about the strategies used and why they worked. These can be the most powerful lessons.

Make transition.

A basic idea in anger management is that anger starts, is maintained, and is fueled by the self-statements we make when we are provoked to anger. A basic way of gaining control is to change what we're saying to ourselves—changing our anger-producing self-statements to anger-controlling ones. Let's do some more work on that today, this time for some of the tougher situations when we're already angry and for after we have shown our anger.

Reinforce the Quieting Response.

Before we start, this might be a good time to do the QR together.

Take in a deep breath. Push out your abdomen with it and hold it. Now slowly let it out to the count of ten:

1 . . . 2 . . . 3 . . . 4 . . . 5 . . . 6 . . . 7 . . . 8 . . . 9 . . . 10

Good job! Now lean forward, shake yourself loose of body tensions, and let's practice it again.

Link experience to next steps.

Remember, the QR is especially important for handling triggers and troublemakers—to keep you from responding impulsively and "losing your cool." It's going to be important to use it liberally in Stage 3, when we're already angry, in order to get a grip on our anger.

2. Self-Talk to Control Anger

Introduce, explain.

Introduce the continuation of this exercise and the purpose for it. For example:

Even though we can inoculate ourselves against anger and use strategies to prevent losing our cool, the fact is that sometimes, when confronted with people or events that provoke us, we sort of move right into automatic pilot and choose to get angry.

Hand out Self-Talk Examples to Rehearse for Controlling Anger (Stages 3 and 4)

Have students focus on the self-talk used for the next two anger stages: coping when already angry and reflecting after the event.

We targeted Stages 1 and 2 last time. This time we're working with Stages 3 and 4. The purpose is to come up with self-talk examples we can commit to using, ones that fit us.

Group works on task.

Have students work in groups of two or three.

Ask them to select examples for the "during" and "after" stages that they could see themselves using. Also have them select those that they just couldn't use for one reason or another.

Ask them to record on a sheet of paper any additional statements that they would use, ones that achieve the same purposes as those listed in the handout.

Group shares, makes decisions, commits to practice.

When each small group is finished, reconvene the large group and have students report their results to the total group.

Finally, compare the new scripts generated with the Self-Talk Examples handout to see: 1) if their additions are communicating the same central message and are in the same spirit and 2) which ones the group votes on to add to the handout. (Note: Be sure to follow-up by having the list retyped to reflect their additions and give everyone a copy at the next session.)

Ask each person to select two statements for each stage, ones that they will commit to using with one of their specific triggers. Next, go around the circle and have everyone report their choices.

Record the most-favored choices on the flip chart and report these back to the group as a way of summarizing.

Foster group culture.

Tell the students that these choices are important for everyone to remember, to use as a kind of "group culture." Reinforce statements that all can subscribe to and delete those that none of them would ever use.

3. Coping with Anger—A Scripting Strategy

Introduce applying self-talk to specific triggers and troublemakers.

One way of learning to control anger is to develop new scripts. We've talked about our personal triggers and troublemakers. I've posted the most common ones we identified (refer to poster).

Now we're going to start to work on controlling ourselves when we already are angry and in danger of losing control.

Have group members recall one of their specific triggers or troublemakers (a relatively simple one) to use in learning the skills and experiencing success.

Group shares.

Ask students what the results usually have been for losing their cool in their situation. For example, looking foolish, making the situation worse, getting grounded or suspended, hurting someone, regretting the behavior, or losing a chance or anopportunity.

Again, foster group sharing and have one of the students record the group's statements on the flip chart.

5. C O P I N G with Anger

Make transition, introduce.

Let's talk about and learn a way of remembering how to put anger-management strategies together so that they are easy to retrieve from our memory bank.

Hand out C O P I N G with Anger: The Steps.

Instruct.

Explain each of the C O P I N G steps in turn.

C = Calm down:
Count to 10. This prepares you to think more clearly. This is a very important first step; if it is ignored, it may be too late to use the rest of the skill.

O = Overcome the negative; Opt for control:
Have students discuss and complete the sentence: "If I lose control now, then _____."

P = Prepare, Problem-solve, Plan:
Point out that this is a crucial moment; they may need to do another QR to think clearly.

I = Identify and invite alternatives. Instead of insults, imagine success:
Say that by this time, if they've used the first three steps successfully, they've got things under control. But they still need to go further and make the situation better. This means taking the last two steps.

N = Name your feelings; Negotiate:
Point out that naming the feeling (anger) can be a signal, a reminder to negotiate instead of blowing up. Negotiating is critical to making things better, improving the typical consequences.

G = Go! Get on with the plan:
Get the hang of anger management.
Give praise to yourself and others.

Group discusses.

Engage students in discussion and in thinking of examples. More important, engage them in selecting and committing to self-talk they can use in their situations (recorded on the index cards in their notebook and as a group profile on the Common Triggers and Troublemakers poster).

Encourage use of the self-talk they selected for their particular situation from the self-statements handout for use in this exercise.

Dyad practice.

Have students work in pairs and list, from their own experiences, steps they took toward anger and losing control. Then have them rewrite their story, using the C O P I N G method they just learned, deciding what they will do and say to themselves to stay in control.

Group shares, gains insight.

Reconvene the larger group. Foster sharing of their rewritten stories. Seek out examples from each student.

Encourage students to listen carefully and to identify the specific coping strategies used in the "rewritten" stories. Ask for a volunteer to record these on the flip chart.

Ask for a summary of the insights they gained. Use the Today...I Discovered that I... poster or strategy.

Follow up with specific observations that make you proud of their work and progress.

5. Reinforce Guided Imagery

This might be a good time to repeat the guided imagery exercise (see page 96) to foster a positive mood and sense of well-being for group members.

6. S T O M P on it!—Another Coping Strategy

Make transition, introduce.

Let's talk about and try out a specific problem-solving strategy, one that will help in the first three steps of the C O P I N G model.

It's a decision-making tool that can help a lot, not only when we're angry but also in the "before" and "after" stages.

It's called S T O M P—a name that helps us think of the fact that we can and have to take action. When we have a decision to make and when we're in the "heat of the moment," then S T O M P on it!

Hand out S T O M P—A Decision-Making Model.

Instruct

Explain each of the S T O M P steps in turn.

S = Stop:
Count to 10. Do a QR.
Do not do something impulsive that could hurt you or others.

T = Think:
Acting on impulse could get me into a heap of trouble!
I can handle this a better way!

O = Options:
What are my options here? Make a list.
Opt to throw out those not helpful, the hurtful ones.
Opt for one that is helpful for me and others.

M = Move on it:
Act on the helpful option you picked.
Try it, don't just think about it.
Rehearse with a friend beforehand, if possible, to increase the chances for success.

P = Praise:
Pat yourself on the back. You S T O M Ped on it!
Positively reinforce yourself and the other person in the situation for giving it a try, for practicing anger control.

Group Exercises S T O M P.

Roll out the piece of butcher paper with the S T O M P words. Ask someone to stand on the word "STOP." Ask two other students to be coaches, to stand on either side of the volunteer, holding the person firmly by the upper arms.

Now, ask for a volunteer to be the "provoker." Instruct him or her and the rest of the group in their parts. The provoker's role is to taunt the volunteer, to provoke him or her into getting mad. Help them get their "script together." Each time the provoker calls out something, the rest of the group yells, "Yeah, how about that!" Coach the group along.

Show the helpers that their job is to get the volunteer to STOP, to count to 10 or to do the QR.

Ready, Go! The provoker starts it. The group yells, "Yeah, yeah!" The volunteer makes a motion toward the provoker as if he or she is going to fight. The two helpers respond by tugging backward on the student's arms, shouting "STOP!" each time the volunteer is provoked and attempts to move forward. The volunteer stops and does a QR, counting to 10 as suggested. The volunteer even invites the provoker, saying, "Hey, let's stop a minute here and count to 10 before we lose our cool."

The helpers now move the student to "THINK." Thank the provoker for his or her role and thank the helpers for doing a great job at helping the volunteer STOP.

Engage the group in walking the person through each step of S T O M P. The whole group now takes on a supportive role for the next steps.

Ask for two new helpers to take a turn at coaching the volunteer in the "THINK" step. Thank them for doing a great coaching job. Move the volunteer to the "OPTIONS" position and name two new helpers as coaches.

At the "OPTIONS" position, have one coach engage the volunteer in thinking of three or four options for responding. Have the other coach jot down the options on the flip chart. Have the group help the coach and volunteer think of options. List the options and ask the group to consider whether options are helpful or not. The coaches move the volunteer appropriately to either the "Not Helpful" or "Helpful" positions on the butcher paper. Thank the coaches and group for a job well done and move the volunteer to the next position.

Repeat the process with the "MOVE ON IT" step. The volunteer is engaged, with the help of the coach and group, to consider what it will take to carry out the chosen action. Finally, the volunteer moves to the "PRAISE" step, where self-praise is carried out and the volunteer is cheered by the group.

Note: It is important to orchestrate this learning opportunity at a good pace so that the group does not get bogged down. This is an example of the kind of action-oriented learning that students enjoy. It gets them out of their seats, moving around, participating, and engaged in learning in a fun way.

It will be important to have the group practice S T O M P using other issues and student volunteers in ensuing sessions so that everyone has the opportunity to learn and apply the skill.

Part III: Wrapping It Up

1. Summarize, Promote Insight, Personalize

Guide the group through closure.

- Ask some of the students to summarize major points.

- Check for comprehension.

- Check for personalization. Use the Today...I Discovered that... poster.

- Model the skills in your own behavior.

Reinforce and praise by sharing specifics you observed in skill development for each individual and in the group's work and peer support.

Model, model, model the support and skills in your own behavior.

2. Promote "Taking It Away!"

- Have each student commit to show a friend outside the group how to do the QR between now and the next group, or

- Have each student name and commit to a specific situation in which they will do the QR and use specific self-talk examples.

- Inspire:

To make these skills a natural part of our behavior, we have to use and practice them.

- Tell the students:

On the top of next session's agenda will be "Check-In," reports of our success stories from this coming week. And we'll continue applying and practicing C O P I N G and S T O M P during our next session.

It will important to make sure that everyone gets a chance to practice using C O P I N G and S T O M P, using the common triggers and troublemakers we've identified. So during the week, think about some of your specific situations and rehearse the steps. Come to our next group knowing each step in C O P I N G and S T O M P. It also would be great if you'd practice using some of the scripts that you think would work for you.

Part IV: Monitoring/Check-Back Activities

Student commitments to remember are:

Student's Name   Commitments Made

_____

_____

_____

_____

_____

_____

_____

_____

_____

_____

_____

See also the Appendix for sample TTFBC check-back tools to use.

Guided Self-Analysis

Review the videotape of your group session.

Using the lists of Leader Competencies from Chapter 1, complete the following:

Leader Competencies for Fostering the Group-Support System

Examples of strengths in fostering group support I observed were:

1. _____

2. _____

3. _____

4. _____

5. _____

A growth objective to work on next time is:

_____

_____

Leader Competencies for Fostering the Skills-Training Component

Examples of strengths in skills training I observed were:

1. _____

2. _____

3. _____

4. _____

5. _____

A growth objective to work on next time is:

_____

_____

I am particularly proud of:

_____

_____

SELF-TALK EXAMPLES TO REHEARSE FOR CONTROLLING ANGER
Stages 3 and 4

(Adapted from Novaco, 1975)

Coping when I'm already angry or starting "to fume"

My muscles are starting to tense. Do the QR! Slow things down.

"Catastrophizing" won't help. Think straight!

I'm angry; that's a signal of what I need to do. Time to instruct myself.

Lower the tone, lower the volume, speak slower.

Getting upset won't help. It gets me into trouble.

Negatives lead to more negatives. Work constructively.

Reason it out. Take the issue point by point.

Try the cooperative approach. Maybe we're both right.

Ask that we treat each other with respect.

I can't expect people to act the way I want them to.

Take it easy, don't get pushy! Negotiate.

Reflecting—after the event

a. When conflict is unresolved

Forget about it. Thinking about it makes you more upset.

Don't stretch the situation into awful.

This is a difficult situation that will take time to heal.

Try to shake it off. Don't let it outweigh the positives.

Remember the relaxation exercise. It's better than depression.

Can you laugh about it? It's probably not so serious.

Don't take it personally. You did the best you could, better than last time!

It takes two to resolve things. You did your part!

I'll get better at this with more practice.

b. When conflict is resolved or coping is successful

I handled that pretty well. It worked!

That wasn't as hard as I thought.

It could have been a lot worse. Nice going!

I could have gotten more upset than it was worth.

I actually got through that without "losing my cool."

My pride gets me into trouble; but when I don't "blow it," I'm better off.

I guess I've been getting upset for too long when it wasn't even necessary.

I'm getting better at this all the time.

C O P I N G WITH ANGER: THE STEPS
(and KEY SELF-TALK PHRASES)

C = CALM DOWN!
(Say: "Calm down! STOP! Do the QR.")

or _____

_____

O = OVERCOME THE NEGATIVE; OPT FOR CONTROL.
(Say: "Overcome — the desire to blow things out of proportion! This isn't necessarily AWFUL, DREADFUL, TERRIBLE! Easy does it! I'm in control, I can handle this!")

or _____

_____

P = PREPARE, PROBLEM-SOLVE, PLAN.
(Say: "Think! Problem-solve, remember your plan, don't get pushy!)

or _____

_____

I = IDENTIFY, INVITE ALTERNATIVES INSTEAD OF USING INSULTS.
(Say: "Imagine success; don't assume the worst. If I start to get mad, I'll just be banging my head against the wall. Don't use insults.")

or _____

_____

N = NAME THE ANGER FEELINGS; NEGOTIATE.
(Say: "I'm angry; that's a signal to think about negotiation. Remember, negatives lead to more negatives. Negotiation can lead to win-win situations.")

or _____

_____

G = GO! GET ON WITH THE PLAN! GET THE HANG OF ANGER MANAGEMENT! GIVE PRAISE TO SELF and OTHERS.
(Say: "Way to go! Good job! Nice going to both of us! Thanks for negotiating and helping me with my anger control!")

or _____

_____

S T O M P—A Decision-Making Model*

S = **STOP** — Do a QR

T = **THINK** — I can handle this

O = **OPTIONS** — Brainstorm

Then Evaluate and List as:
A. NOT HELPFUL   vs.   B. HELPFUL
(discard!)   (select one)

M = **MOVE ON IT** — Do it!

Act on your selected option

P = **PRAISE** — A pat on the back!

You S T O M Ped On It!

*Adapted from Gordon Dickman's *Stomp,* Personal Growth Class Project 06/90

Module 5

Applying Anger Control at Home, School, and Work and in Personal Relationships

I. Background

Brief Description of the Module

This module is designed as the primary skills application and practice component of *Anger Management for Youth*. Suggested exercises involve multiple options for activities in the "skill center" and "practice field" shown on the Anger-Management Trip Map. The focus is on practice, practice, and more practice, involving:

- rehearsal with personal triggers and troublemakers,

- "play-back" analyses,

- group feedback/support, and

- support contracts.

Learning Objectives

During and after the learning activities presented in this module, students will:

1. Practice taking control with their specific triggers and troublemakers.

2. Practice thought refocusing and self-talk for specific anger-provoking situations.

3. Practice using relaxation techniques—QR and guided imagery.

4. Solve problems and rehearse C O P I N G with anger strategies for specific trigger situations involving teachers, friends, antagonists, and family members.

5. Conduct "play-back" analyses of both successful and unsuccessful conflict resolutions.

6. Enlist support from family, friends, teachers, and classmates for gaining control of anger.

Training Level

(X indicates those that apply to this module)

___ Skills Assessment   ___ Skills Acquisition
_X_ Skills Application   _X_ Skills Monitoring/Check-Backs

Leader Strategies

The leader will need to use the full range of competencies for fostering a strong group support system for the exercises in this module. Setting this stage is critical for skills application by the students. For these skills to become a natural part of their repertoire, they need a lot of practice. When this practice occurs in a nonthreatening, supportive environment, there likely will be less reticence and discomfort by the students.

Review the leader role competencies in Chapter 2 before proceeding with this module. In addition to encouraging and fostering a culture of caring within the group, the leader is expected to use the full range of skills-training competencies in order to make the learning opportunities appealing to the students. These are:

_X_ Instruction	_X_ Game
_X_ Modeling	_X_ Questionnaire/Scale
_X_ Group Discussion	_X_ Group Exercise
_X_ Group Practice	_X_ Role Play
_X_ Indiv/Dyad Practice	_X_ Real Life Assignment
_X_ Homework	___ Other: _____

Attachments

1. Self-Talk Examples to Rehearse for Controlling Anger (for Stages 1-4) (page 129)

2. Some Ways of Replacing Anger—Discussion Outline (page 130)

3. Role Rehearsal Situations for Anger-Management Training (page 131)

4. Gift Cards and Gift Certificates (pages xx)

Leader Preparations

Materials needed and things to do ahead of time include:

1. Handouts/Teacher Guides

   a. Some Ways of Replacing Anger—Discussion Outline (review).

   b. Role Rehearsal Situations for Anger-Management Training (Review and choose options to use; make copies for students if called for).

   c. Gift Cards and Gift Certificates (make copies for each student of those you plan to use).

   d. Sample TTFBC check-back tools to use as appropriate (make a copy for each student).

2. Posters, Overheads to Make

   a. Anger-Management Trip Map. "Practice Field" is now the focus, so highlight that on the poster).

   b. S T O M P

   c. C O P I N G with anger.

   d. Self-Talk Examples to Rehearse (Stages 1 to 4: retype to add students' additions and deletions from the last session and make a copy for each student).

3. Review Monitoring and Check-Back Notes; Review for any Materials Needed from Previous Sessions

   a. Students' index cards of personal triggers and troublemakers; these should be in their binders.

   b. Handouts or posters from Modules 1 to 4.

4. Review Growth Objectives from Previous Self-Analysis

   a. Make specific plans to implement group-support objective. Write this into your implementation plans.

   b. Similarly, make specific plans to implement the skills-training objective.

5. Set up equipment for video taping session.

Implementation Guidelines

Part I: Motivational Preparation

Recall the purpose is to motivate, to invite, to instill hope and promise. Again, this means you

- Reveal objectives in an interesting manner.

- Promote the perceived purpose.

- Describe the strategies as appealing and valuable.

1. Inspire, Motivate

Provide positive feedback for the fine work accomplished in the prior session. Review your notes and be prepared to give concrete examples of what you observed that showed real growth in maturity and behavior change. Give positive feedback equally to all students. (See Part II, #8, Leader Praise, on page 125 for more specific guidelines.)

2. Reveal Objectives

Refer to the Anger-Management Trip Map poster. Point out:

We're in the "Practice Field." Look, we've come a long way and we're close to reaching our goal.

Our objectives in the "practice field" are to experience:

- *daily self-talk workouts,*

- *a lot of role-play practice,*

- *direct experience with our triggers and troublemakers, and*

- *a lot of group support.*

3. Reinforce Perceived Purposes

To reach our goal of "permanent membership" in the Anger Control Center!

To promote getting along better with friends, family, and future loved ones by achieving anger control, that is, by keeping expressions of anger at manageable and nondestructive levels.

4. Reinforce How We Continue Growth at This Stage

By setting goals for practicing specific behavior changes.

By contracting for support and for feedback on skills.

By experiencing the rewards of new behaviors in personal relationships with friends, with teachers, with family, etc.

By beginning to tackle some of the bigger troublemakers with the skills we learned and practiced on simpler issues.

By practice, practice, practice of new behaviors in order to become competent and sophisticated so that the skills become a natural part of us.

Most important, by monitoring and tracking our progress, our successes, and our achievements along our Anger-Management Trip.

Last session we focused on strategies for _____.
(This will change for each session in this module.)

Today, we're going to focus on strategies for _____.

5. An Option for One of the Sessions.

The Ways of Replacing Anger Discussion Outline may be useful as a stimulus and review during one of your group sessions in this module.

Part II: Learning Activities/Process Guidelines

What follows in this module are a range of learning activities that capitalize on the skills building already completed. Select one or two activities per session for practice and refinement of the skills. Note, it is not the intention that you and your group attempt to cover all the learning activities in this module within one session. This would not be possible, because everyone in the group needs appropriate practice time and opportunities for feedback from the group.

A reminder of your leadership role:

- Provide for large doses of group support.

- Provide appropriate practice for everyone.

- Provide for "check-backs" to monitor progress.

- Provide for relevant positive feedback; instruct and engage students in using specific examples.

- Model the skills in your own behavior.

1. Monitoring and Check-Backs

Self-monitoring.

Instruct in the use of a self-monitoring tool from the Appendix. Use systematically and combine with positive reinforcers.

Group sharing, summary of insights gained

Hand out your retyped, revised version of Self-Talk Examples to Rehearse for Controlling Anger. This version includes their additions and deletions.

Use "Check-In" procedure to get reports of success stories about implementing their use of the self-talk, QR, C O P I N G and S T O M P strategies.

Summarize the group discussion of the insights they gained. Point out the skills they used and provide insights about the strategies and why they worked. These can be the most powerful lessons.

2. Support Contracts—Gift Cards and Gift Certificates

Students develop support contracts.

Have each student develop a support contract with the group members. Negotiate appropriate rewards.

(See Gift Cards and Gift Certificates on pages 135-137.)

Repeat.

Repeat the above step for working through anger control with a significant other, a teacher, and a parent or guardian.

3. Self-Exploration (Imagery) Individual Exercises

Students continue working on index cards.

They order these situations into hierarchies, identify their anger-related self-statements in each situation, apply the C O P I N G model to the specific situation, and rehearse to prepare for these provocations.

Group discusses, reasons together.

Continue to have students gain insights into their reasons for using anger with each trigger and troublemaker:

- Use Why You Choose Anger: 12 Typical Motives (page 94).

- Ask each student to look over the list and place a check mark next to the reasons they used anger in the anger situation they just relived.

4. Self-Talk Inoculations: A Coping Strategy

Use Self-Talk Examples to Rehearse for Controlling Anger for 1) "before" buttons are pushed, 2) "when first" triggered, 3) when coping with arousal, and 4) during "play-back."

Continue to refine this handout.

Foster a group culture and norms of responses most acceptable to all.

The goal in this scripting is to make these "lines" easy to remember and repeat and to develop ones that the individual students feel good about using.

5. The C O P I N G Model—A Scripting Strategy

This model goes hand-in-hand with Self-Talk Inoculations and the S T O M P model. Many different exercises can be designed for practice with pairs, triads, or the larger group.

C = Calm down:
Count to 10. This prepares you to think more clearly. This is a very important first step. If it is ignored, it may be too late to use the rest of the skill.

O = Overcome the negative; Opt for control:
Have students discuss and complete the sentence: "If I lose control now, then _____."

P = Prepare, Problem-solve, Plan:
Point out that this is a crucial point in time; they may need to do another QR to think clearly.

I = Identify and invite alternatives. Instead of insults, imagine success:
Say that by this time, if they've used the first three steps successfully, they've got things under control. But they still need to go further and make the situation better. This means taking the last two steps.

N = Name your feelings; Negotiate:
Point out that naming the feeling (anger) can be a signal, a reminder to negotiate instead of blowing up. Negotiating is critical to making things better and improving the consequences.

G = Go! Get on with the plan:
Get the hang of anger management.
Give praise to yourself and others for doing your part.

Success-story practice using C O P I N G.

Have students work in pairs to identify a success story, writing out the things they said in a personal anger-provoking experience.

Have them identify the steps they took toward anger control.

Then have them edit and improve their story, using the C O P I N G with anger method and the self-talk statements.

Follow this with reports to the total group.

Applying C O P I N G to triggers and troublemakers.

Use the C O P I N G model to work through one of the group-identified common triggers and troublemakers. This activity fulfills your promise to the group of systematically getting to their "real-life" issues.

Combine this activity with role-play practice.

(See Role Rehearsal Situations for Anger-Management Trainings on page 131.)

6. Using S T O M P with Role Rehearsal

Group produces situations for practice.

Have students identify anger-provoking situations they experience with teachers, with family, with friends, and with antagonists.

Role rehearsals.

Make a poster of the students' situations.

Work on one per session, using cognitive and role-play rehearsals to have students apply anger-control coping strategies and self-talk scripts for these situations.

See Role Rehearsal Situations for Anger-Management Training on page 131 for ideas and directions.

7. Relaxation Techniques

QR practice.

Begin and end each session with the Quieting Response. Ensure that each student leads the group in this exercise at least once during this module, and more often if possible.

Have the group do the QR any time during the group sessions when things get tense.

Guided-imagery practice.

Take the group on a trip to their island, using the Guided Imagery script whenever appropriate (e.g., if they come into group tense or hyperactive) and whenever they request it.

Have students lead the group in variations on this theme that they use for relaxation and a sense of well-being.

8. Reinforcement Options for Anger-Management Training.

1. Identifying strategies used, praise.

Have each student identify a success story in using one or more strategies in anger control. Have group members identify the strategy used in each case, and give the student praise.

2. Leader praise, "strength bombardments."

Identify ahead of time specific things you've observed each student do and say where you think they should be proud of growth and progress made in effort, internal responsibility, and anger control. Don't try to do this "off the cuff." Take time to prepare this ahead of class, and then go around the circle with at least one item per student. Vary this activity, sometimes giving the feedback verbally and, at other times, writing these in "You should be proud" cards or inserting them into fortune cookies or some other means whereby the group members have this feedback in writing.

3. Group praise, positive reinforcements.

Have each student take time to identify and report the growth in exercising anger or depression management that they have observed in the person sitting next to them. This will take your leadership in order for it to be a powerful experience, and it may need to be done in several stages as follows:

Ask each student to share an anger-control goal they are willing to work on in the group; then have each student complete the Gift Card Pay to Group Members. Also, have each student negotiate an appropriate reward that the group will provide when the student meets his or her anger-control goal. These rewards can then be transferred onto the Gift Certificates, which indicate that the reward will be paid to the bearer when he or she successfully meets his or her anger-control goal in *Anger Management for Youth*.

Post the Gift Cards and Gift Certificates in the room.

Ask each student to observe the person next to them for a week for evidence of goal achievement.

Ask for reports after a day or two and then again at the end of the week (or whatever period of time negotiated by the group). Be firm during reports and do not let them get negative. Also, be prepared to provide additional evidence as needed if the observer is absent or needs assistance with his or her task. Distribute Gift Certificates as earned.

4. *Group identifies desired support, reinforcement.*

Ask each group member to identify how they would like to be supported and praised—the specific actions that would be most meaningful to them. Record these, model using them, and engage group members in remembering and using them with each other.

Keep track of multiple ways of making reinforcement from you and the group both genuine and specific. This is the essence of social support.

5. *"Bring and brag."*

Establish a "bring and brag" routine at the beginning of each group session. This is a time for group members to automatically report back to the group a strategy that they tried, a success they had, and some "points they made." The group responds each time for each person with enthusiastic applause.

Part III: Wrapping It Up

1. Summarize, Promote Insight, Personalize

Guide the group through closure.

- Ask some of the students to summarize major points.
- Check for comprehension.
- Check for personalization. Use the Today...I discovered that... poster.
- Model the skills in your own behavior.

Reinforce and praise by sharing specifics you observed in skill development for each individual and in the group's work and peer support!

Model, model, model the support and skills in your own behavior.

2. Promote "Taking It Away!"

- Have each student commit to practicing a specific skill covered in the group with a friend, a teacher, and so forth. Work from simple situations to the more difficult ones.
- Inspire:

To make these skills a natural part of our behavior, we have to use them, practice them, and then apply them over and over.

Part IV: Monitoring/Check-Back Activities

Things to check-back on next session are:

Student's Name   Commitments Made

_____

_____

_____

_____

_____

_____

_____

_____

_____

_____

_____

_____

Guided Self-Analysis

Review the videotape of your group session.

Using the lists of Leader Competencies from Chapter 1, complete the following:

Leader Competencies for Fostering the Group-Support System

Examples of strengths in fostering group support I observed were:

1. _____
2. _____
3. _____
4. _____
5. _____

A growth objective to work on next time is:

_____

_____

Leader Competencies for Fostering the Skills-Training Component

Examples of strengths in skills training I observed were:

1. _____
2. _____
3. _____
4. _____
5. _____

A growth objective to work on next time is:

_____

_____

I am particularly proud of:

_____

_____

SELF-TALK EXAMPLES TO REHEARSE
FOR CONTROLLING ANGER

(Adapted from Novaco, 1975)

1. Preparing for "Anger Triggers" — things that "push my button"

This is going to be upsetting, but I can handle it.
This doesn't have to be a catastrophe.
Stop! Figure out what I have to do...work out a plan.
I can manage this. I know how to control my anger.
I'll know what to do if I find myself getting upset:
   relax, take a deep breath, remember my plan.
Don't overreact. Don't blow this out of proportion.
This could be a sticky situation, but I believe in myself.
Time for the QR. Feel comfortable, relaxed, at ease.
Easy does it. Remember to keep your sense of humor.
Easy does it. Remember your lines.

2. When confronted, when my "button is pushed"

Stop! Stay calm. Think! Don't jump to conclusions.
Do the QR, or count to 10.
Don't blow things out of proportion.
So it hurts! There's no use stretching it into an
   Awful, Dreadful, Terrible situation.
As long as I keep my cool, I'm in control.
Don't get bent out of shape. Stick with the plan.
I don't need to prove myself. I know I am O.K.
There is no point in getting out of control.
Don't make more of this than I have to.
Look for the positives. Don't assume the worst.
If I start to get mad, I'll just be banging my head
   against the wall. So I might as well just relax.
There is no need to doubt myself. I can handle this!
I'm on top of the situation, and it's under control.

3. Coping when I'm already angry or starting "to fume"

My muscles are starting to tense. Do the QR! Slow
things down.
"Catastrophizing" won't help. Think straight!
I'm angry...that's a signal of what I need to do.
   Time to instruct myself.
Lower the tone, lower the volume, speak slower.
Getting upset won't help. It gets me into trouble.
Negatives lead to more negatives. Work constructively.
Reason it out. Take the issue point by point.
Try the cooperative approach. Maybe we're both right.
Ask that we treat each other with respect.
I can't expect people to act the way I want them to.
Take it easy, don't get pushy! Negotiate.

4. Reflecting — after the event.

a. When conflict is unresolved
Forget about it. Thinking about it makes me more
upset. Don't stretch the situation into awful!
This is a difficult situation that will take time to heal.
Try to shake it off. Don't let it outweigh the positives.
Remember relaxation, exercise. It's better than
   depression.
Can I laugh about it? It's probably not so serious.
Don't take it personally. I did the best I could, better
   than last time!
It takes two to resolve things. I did my part!
I'll get better at this with more practice.

b. When conflict is resolved or coping is successful
I handled that pretty well. It worked!
That wasn't as hard as I thought.
It could have been a lot worse. Nice going!
I could have gotten more upset than it was worth.
I actually got through that without "losing my cool"!
My pride gets me into trouble, but when I don't "blow
   it," I'm better off.
I guess I've been getting upset for too long when it
   wasn't even necessary.
I'm getting better at this all the time.

SOME WAYS OF REPLACING ANGER*
DISCUSSION OUTLINE

UNCONTROLLED ANGER CAN BE ELIMINATED! WE CAN CHOOSE TO LEARN NEW FEELINGS AND MORE PRODUCTIVE BEHAVIORS

1. DEFUSE anger by doing something for the first 10 seconds—e.g., a) taking a deep breath and blowing out slowly to the count of 10, b) naming how you feel and reminding yourself that is a signal to "cool it," and c) labeling how the other person might be feeling. Note: The first 10 seconds are crucial to gaining control!

2. POSTPONE anger explosions. Start by postponing them 15 seconds, then 20 seconds, then 30 seconds, and so on. Keep extending your time before exploding. Postponing is learned control; with practice, this eliminates explosions.

3. REMEMBER that anger doesn't have to be a "natural" response. Getting angry less often is healthier. Expressing anger appropriately (as irritation, disappointment, etc.) is better than storing it up.

4. REMIND YOURSELF that 50% of what you believe should be will be rejected by 50% of others 50% of the time. Once you expect others to disagree you'll choose anger less often. So, get rid of the unrealistic expectations you have for others—your "shoulds" for them. When they go away, so will much of your anger.

   STOP! at the moment of choosing anger! Remind yourself everyone has a right to be as they choose. Demanding that others be and respond as *you want* will simply prolong your anger.

5. GET IN TOUCH with your thoughts when provoked. Remind yourself that you do not have to think that way (i.e., this is awful, terrible, shouldn't be, etc.). Awareness is a most important beginning.

6. GET HELP from someone you trust. Negotiate to have them send you a signal when they see your anger. When you get the signal, think about what you're doing and switch gears to what you planned to do instead—then DO IT!

7. WHEN YOU EXPLODE or have a temper tantrum (or give someone the silent treatment, etc.), STOP! Speak up and tell someone about your SLIP—that your goal is to think and behave differently. Owning up to your "slips" keeps you in touch with yourself and demonstrates that you're working on yourself and your anger issues.

8. TALK to the person who usually gets the "short end of your fuse." Share with each other the most anger-provoking triggers and troublemakers. Plan a way of communicating irritation or frustration without destructive anger—for example, writing a note, taking a "cool off" walk together, or using planned scripts to stop yourselves from continuing to abuse each other and experiencing senseless anger.

9. AVOID TRIGGERS! DISTRACT YOURSELF. For example, in traffic jams, instead of yelling, giving someone the finger, etc., use this time creatively—use relaxation strategies, daydream, listen to soothing music, relive exciting or pleasant experiences you've had, plan for other pleasant activities.

10. LOVE YOURSELF! When you do, you won't burden yourself with self-destructive anger. Get a sense of humor—it's impossible to be angry and laugh at the same time.

11. USE SITUATIONS FOR PERSONAL GROWTH! Instead of being an emotional slave to frustrating triggers and troublemakers, use these situations as a challenge to change, to grow!

12. KEEP A DIARY or journal. Record all angry behaviors you've chosen, and record your successes at anger control. The very act of recording will a) persuade you to choose anger less often and b) reinforce your successes. Try it! (See pages 143-144.)

*Adapted from Dyer, W. (1977) Farewell to Anger, in *Your Erroneous Zones*. NY: Avon Books.

ROLE REHEARSAL SITUATIONS FOR ANGER-MANAGEMENT TRAINING

IMPORTANT PRINCIPLES ARE:

- START WITH SIMPLE "TRIGGERS" FIRST; TRY TO GUARANTEE SUCCESS.
- USE GENEROUS DOSES OF INDIVIDUAL AND GROUP POSITIVE FEEDBACK.
- DEFINE SITUATIONS AS PROBLEMS THAT CALL FOR SOLUTIONS RATHER THAN AS THREATS CALLING FOR ATTACK.
- FOCUS ON THE ISSUES INVOLVED; AVOID RESPONDING IN ANGER.

SOME OPTIONS:

1. **USE STUDENTS' IDENTIFIED SITUATIONS**. The very best role rehearsals are those that the students have identified in the earlier sessions. Have students sort their index cards and group those related to 1) this group, 2) school and teachers, 3) work, 4) friends, and 5) family. These situations can be arranged hierarchically—from simple TRIGGERS to most difficult TROUBLEMAKERS. Remember: Work with simple triggers first and leave the troublemakers (usually dealing with family) until students have developed skills and experienced success.

Work with one or two of these each week. Become familiar with the situations students have on their index cards; then you can integrate anger-management training as these issues come up in group discussions and sharing of issues.

Process:

- Ask for or suggest a situation from the students' experiences.
- Assign roles. The student rehearsing, an antagonist, two coaches, and group observers. Have the student who is rehearsing anger-control responses select two people to be his or her coach. Initially, you can assume the role of coach to model the behavior and guarantee success. The coach's role is to be an "alter ego" for the student as he or she is being provoked.
- Have the student enact coping strategies. Those to promote here are:
    - The C O P I N G sequence—(see C O P I N G with Anger worksheet on page 114)
    - Self-statements to rehearse in anger-provoking situations (use the handout for coaches).
    - Appropriate verbal and nonverbal behaviors.
- Assign the group to observe the person practicing the skills. They need to be prepared to give positive feedback regarding the use of self-talk, C O P I N G skills, and appropriate verbal and nonverbal behaviors.
- Feedback after role rehearsal should include specific behaviors observed. Also use "play-back" analysis and self-talk statements for a) when conflict is unresolved and b) when conflict is resolved or coping is successful. Focus heavily on the positive!

2. **USE STUDENTS' SUCCESS STORIES/SITUATIONS.** As soon as possible, have students bring success stories to the group. Call for a volunteer to report a situation where they used the skills. Play this out! This can be like a "re-run" or "re-play" and can be acted out. This reinforces the skills training and can be a powerful experience.

Keep the role play or discussion going as long as it is lively. Ask students to identify the coping strategies used, that is, self-talk for thought refocusing, relaxation techniques, sticking to the students' plan, problem-solving/negotiation behaviors, appropriate verbal/nonverbal behaviors. This will take your leadership if it is to be a powerful experience. The student enacting his or her success demonstrates the skills and gets positive feedback, and the students observing learn vicariously.

IN GROUP*

A. **On Friday during group when you're going over the weekly attendance, another student confronts you with not being honest in your ratings. You claimed that you were getting to 5th period class every day, but she tells the group you were skipping because she was too and saw you out of class.**

1. She says that you are hurting yourself by lying about your class attendance. She says she is skipping too, but not lying about it. How could you behave and what could you say while keeping your anger and defensiveness under control?

2. Describe how the group could behave and what people could say to let you know that skipping is not the main issue, personal responsibility is the issue; and as members of the group, that is their business and concern.

B. **A particular member of the group is monopolizing group time and often will not cooperate with the group's wishes. She threatens to leave if she doesn't get her way, and she frequently is angry when challenged.**

1. What could our group members say and do to help this group member deal with her anger-control problem?

2. Describe the various options the group could use to resolve this conflict successfully.

FRIENDS**

A. **One of your friends likes a girl named Debbie, but they're not going steady. You think she's pretty great yourself. You went out with her Saturday night, and you both had a really good time. Someone must have told your friend, because he comes running up to you outside school and says, "You dirty rat! Bill just told me about you and Debbie. I'm gonna knock your ugly face in!" What do you say and do now?**

B. **The girl you've been going with just broke up with you. She said that you're O.K., but she would like to go out with other guys, too. You still care about her, and you're hurt and angry that she doesn't want to continue to be your girl. You're in a terrible, miserable mood. You feel really down.**

1. What could you say and do to deal with your girlfriend?

2. How could you go about getting out of your bad mood—depression, anger?

C. You're at a party, and all the kids there are smoking pot. You used to do a lot of pot smoking yourself, but now you've quit because you got busted and made a commitment to do so in group. Everyone knows you used to smoke. Your girlfriend offers you a joint; and when you say "no thanks," she makes fun of you for being a "goody-goody." This triggers your anger for a number of reasons.

1. What could you say and do to stick to your "no smoking pot" goal and maintain anger control?

2. Some of your *Anger Management for Youth* friends are also at the party. How could you enlist their help if they had not seen or heard what was happening? If they overheard what was going on, what could they do and say to be supportive to you?

ANTAGONISTS**

A. You're playing basketball in the school yard, and some kids you don't know very well are standing together on the sidelines. They start yelling at you, calling you names, and making fun of the way you play. One of them says, "Hey, look at the tub of lard! Looks like a ball of pizza dough!" What do you say and do?

B. You're about an hour late getting to work at Safeway because your car ran out of gas. You feel stupid about that and are uptight because you know your boss will be mad; and he has a right to be mad, because this is the busiest time of the day in the store. You punch in at the time-clock, and he comes storming over to you and says, "You're fired! I've put up with you kids being late and now showing up one time too many! Starting with you, anyone who comes in late gets canned!" What do you say and do? (You really want to keep this job!)

TEACHERS*

A. You're skipping a particular class too often and also are frequently tardy. The teacher of the class wants you to know three things:

- You're missing important information and not learning it.

- Skipping and being tardy are against school policy.

- You're making the teacher's job harder, because she has to spend extra time preparing make-up work when you're gone and catch you up when you're late; this make her angry.

1. How could the teacher get her messages across to you and get you to take it serious?

2. How can you prevent yourself from becoming angry and defensive? What could you say? What could you do?

3. Of the three teacher messages above, which is your responsibility? All? None? Why?

B. You frequently do not hand in your assignments in this one class. Your teacher obviously is both angry and concerned for your progress, but he seems to avoid confronting you as often as you would expect.

Role Rehearsal Situations (continued)

1) How could he behave and what could he say to let you know that you are hurting your chances of earning credit in the class, hurting your growth to be more responsible, and making the teacher angry. Also, your teacher does not want you to feel picked on.

2) How could you behave and what could you say to let the teacher know that you understand the concern and anger and you will try to get better, but it hurts your feelings that he seems to avoid talking with you about it.

PARENTS*

A. Your mom (or guardian) likes keeping the house clean. You are in a hurry to meet a friend and you leave a mess in the kitchen and leave your clothes, books, and other stuff in the living room. When you get home, your mom is very angry but is working hard to avoid "blowing up" at you.

1. What could you say to avoid triggering a serious, hostile confrontation? What could you say to "own your piece of the pie" here—to let her know you were irresponsible?

2. What could you do to avoid such "anger" encounters in the future?

3. What could your mom do or say to a) let you know she appreciates your intentions and b) to persuade you to take her seriously—that is, to stop leaving your messes around and to clean up after yourself?

B. You're expected home at midnight on a Friday night. You arrive at 2 a.m. without phoning home with an explanation. Your parents were angry and worried.

1. Identify reasons you might have for being late; which are external (outside yourself) and which are internal (taking self-responsibility)?

2. How could your parents explain their anger and worry in ways that would help you from choosing anger and defensiveness? How could you prevent yourself from becoming defensive? What could they say to help you understand their point of view?

3. How could you respond and let your parents know that you understand their message? What could you say to let them know how you could have handled external events better? And what could you say to let them know you are taking personal responsibility for your lateness?

*From Conrath, J. (1986). *Our other youth: Prevention curriculum.* Gig Harbor, WA.

**Adapted from Freedman, B. (1974): A Social-Behavioral Analysis of Skills Deficits in Delinquent and Non-Delinquent Adolescent Boys. [Doctoral dissertation]. University of Wisconsin, Madison.

Gift Card

PAY TO MY FAMILY:

In an Attempt to Fight More Fairly,

I will _____

(Fill in goals for behavior)

_____

_____

Caringly Yours,

_____

Gift Certificate

PAY TO THE BEARER:

I will _____

(Fill in agreed-on reward)

_____

(from family)

_____

FOR SUCCESSFULLY KEEPING
MY ANGER-CONTROL GOAL

_____

(Your Name)

Gift Card
PAY TO:

_____
(specify person's name)

In an Attempt to Fight More Fairly,

*I will*_____
(specify behaviors)

_____

Caringly Yours,

_____
(Your Name)

Gift Certificate

PAY TO THE BEARER:

*I will*_____
(Fill in agreed-on reward)

_____

FOR SUCCESSFULLY KEEPING
MY ANGER-CONTROL GOAL

_____
(Your Name)

Gift Card
PAY TO GROUP MEMBERS:

*In an Attempt to Express my Anger More Appropriately
in this Group, I will*

1 _____

(Fill in Goals, Behaviors)

2 _____

3 _____

Caringly Yours,

_____

(Your Name)

Gift Certificate

PAY TO THE BEARER:

_____

(specify reward, privilege agreed to in group)

_____

FOR SUCCESSFULLY MEETING MY ANGER-CONTROL GOAL IN GROUP

_____

(Your Name)

Monitoring and "Check-Back" Tools

I. Background

Brief Description of the Module

This appendix contains a number of tools that are designed for self-monitoring and for assessing progress during the *Anger Management for Youth* program. Monitoring is a powerful strategy for enhancing self-awareness, staying on track, getting back on track after a "slip," and preventing relapses.

There are tools suitable for each phase of skills training covered in the *Anger Management for Youth* program: self-assessment, skills building, and skills application and practice.

Learning Objectives

By using these tools, students will:

1. Be able to identify their anger triggers and troublemakers.

2. Develop self-awareness of their uncontrolled anger sequences.

3. Identify effective control strategies used in breaking their uncontrolled anger cycle.

4. Personalize the TTFBC process and identify successful changes made in the TTFBC process.

5. Make using C O P I N G strategies a regular habit.

6. Make using the S T O M P model a regular habit.

7. Receive positive reinforcement from the *Anger Management for Youth* group.

8. Check their level of anger control with their triggers and troublemakers.

Leader Strategies

The leader will need to review the tools and decide when to incorporate them into the *Anger Management for Youth* modules.

When using the tools, the leader is expected to encourage and foster a culture of caring within the group in order that the self-disclosures of group members are handled sensitively.

In addition, the leader is expected to use the following skills-training competencies in order to make monitoring beneficial and appealing to the students:

_X_ Instruction	___ Game
_X_ Modeling	_X_ Questionnaire/Scale
_X_ Group Discussion	___ Group Exercise
___ Group Practice	___ Role Play
_X_ Indiv/Dyad Practice	___ Real-Life Assignment
___ Homework	___ Other: _____

Attachments

1. My Typical Anger Triggers & Troublemakers (page 141)

2. TTFBC Check-Up (page 142)

3. My Uncontrolled-Anger-Sequence Diary (page 143)

4. Breaking the Uncontrolled Anger Cycle (page 145)

5. How Are You Doing with Your Anger-Management Program? (page 147)

6. C O P I N G with Anger: Habit Checks (page 148)

7. *S T O M P* on It!: Habit Checks (page 149)

8. Check-In: Anger Control with My Triggers & Troublemakers (page 150)

9. Examples of Reinforcement Options for Anger-Management Training (page 151)

Leader Preparations

Things to think about and do ahead of time include:

1. Review all the tools prior to each session.

2. Decide when you will introduce a particular tool and how you will instruct the students in its use.

3. Make sufficient copies for each student.

4. Practice using the tool yourself before introducing it for use by the students.

5. Plan to have students complete the tool during group whenever possible.

6. Following use of the tool, have each student place it in their three-ring binder behind a divider labeled Monitoring Progress.

7. Whenever you repeat the use of a particular tool, have the students compare the current results with those from previous recordings.

8. Remember: These tools facilitate self-disclosures that need to be respected. If you follow-up the use of the tool with group sharing, give students the opportunity to "pass" if they so choose.

MY TYPICAL ANGER
TRIGGERS & TROUBLEMAKERS*

I GET ANGRY WHEN:	YES	MAYBE	NO
1. Someone lets me down.	____	____	____
2. People are unfair.	____	____	____
3. Something blocks my plans.	____	____	____
4. Someone embarrasses me.	____	____	____
5. I am delayed, held up.	____	____	____
6. I have to take orders from someone.	____	____	____
7. I have to work with incompetent people.	____	____	____
8. I do something stupid!.	____	____	____
9. I don't get credit for what I've done.	____	____	____
10. Someone puts me down.	____	____	____
11. _____ (other)	____	____	____
12. _____ (other)	____	____	____

*Adapted from Seigel, J. (1986). The multidimensional anger inventory. *J. of Personal & Social Psychology, 51*, p. 200.

TTFBC CHECK-UP
HOW ARE YOU DOING?

1. TRIGGERS: What are you currently working on?

2. THOUGHTS: What self-talk are you using for refocusing thought? for stopping anger-producing thought?

3. FEELINGS: How are your thoughts influencing your feelings? How are you doing at anger control?

4. BEHAVIORS: In this situation, what would you like to be able to say or do? How is the practice going?

5. CONSEQUENCES: What consequences have you experienced? How are these different than before?

Name _____ Date _____

MY UNCONTROLLED ANGER SEQUENCE DIARY

Name: _____

DIRECTIONS: Record all angry behaviors you have chosen, and the TTFBCs that go with them. The very act of recording will give you a baseline to work from and, hopefully, will persuade you to choose anger less often. Try it!

DATE	TIME	PLACE	TRIGGER, TROUBLEMAKER	THOUGHTS	FEELINGS	BEHAVIORS	CONSEQUENCES

Name: _____

MY UNCONTROLLED ANGER SEQUENCE DIARY

(continued)

DATE	TIME	PLACE	TRIGGER, TROUBLEMAKER	THOUGHTS	FEELINGS	BEHAVIORS	CONSEQUENCES

Name: _____

BREAKING THE UNCONTROLLED ANGER CYCLE

DIRECTIONS: Record YOUR SUCCESSES at anger control. This should show you your effective strategies and reinforce your successes. Try it! For recording your Anger Level, on a scale of 1 to 5, 1 = not angry, 5 = very angry.

DATE	TIME	PLACE	ANGER TRIGGER	EFFECTIVE CONTROL STRATEGY USED	ANGER LEVEL

Name: _____

BREAKING THE UNCONTROLLED ANGER CYCLE
(continued)

DATE	TIME	PLACE	ANGER TRIGGER	EFFECTIVE CONTROL STRATEGY USED	ANGER LEVEL

HOW ARE YOU DOING WITH YOUR ANGER-MANAGEMENT PROGRAM?
DESCRIBE A SUCCESS STORY

1. TRIGGERS: What "Trigger" or "Troublemaker" did you cope with successfully? What self-talk did you use to prepare yourself for this anger trigger? And what coping strategy did you use when faced with this situation?

2. THOUGHTS: What self-talk did you use for refocusing thought? Did you use any other coping strategies to prevent negative or anger-producing thoughts?

3. FEELINGS: How did you feel? And what did you say to yourself to successfully "keep your cool" and still acknowledge your feelings?

4. BEHAVIORS: What did you do? What did you say? How effective were you?

5. CONSEQUENCES: What were the consequences? Reflecting back, what can you say to yourself now about how you handled the situation?

Name _____   Date _____

COPING WITH ANGER: HABIT CHECKS

WHEN YOUR BUTTON WAS PUSHED, DID YOU . . . .

Week of:

									Total Checks
C = Calm down?									
O = Overcome the negative, opt for control?									
P = Prepare, problem-solve, plan?									
I = Invite alternatives instead of insults?									
N = Name the anger feelings, negotiate?									
G = Get on with the plan? Give praise to yourself and others?									
Total Checks:									

Name: _____

S T O M P on It!: HABIT CHECKS

WHEN YOUR BUTTON WAS PUSHED, DID YOU . . .

Week of:

	Total Checks							
S = STOP (Do a QR)?								
T = THINK (Say, "I can handle this!")?								
O = OPTIONS (Brainstorm and opt for a helpful option)?								
M = MOVE ON IT (Act on your option)?								
P = PRAISE (Give yourself a pat on the back)?								
Total Checks:								

Name: _____

CHECK-IN: ANGER CONTROL
WITH MY TRIGGERS & TROUBLEMAKERS

SUCCESSFULLY TOOK CONTROL
(Check if CONTROL GOAL was achieved)

I GET ANGRY WHEN:

(fill in your triggers/troublemakers)

Date:__/__/__   Date:__/__/__   Date:__/__/__   Date:__/__/__

1. _____   _____   _____   _____   _____

2. _____   _____   _____   _____   _____

3. _____   _____   _____   _____   _____

4. _____   _____   _____   _____   _____

5. _____   _____   _____   _____   _____

6. _____   _____   _____   _____   _____

7. _____   _____   _____   _____   _____

8. _____   _____   _____   _____   _____

9. _____   _____   _____   _____   _____

10. _____   _____   _____   _____   _____

Each scoring session — Fraction attained: _____   _____   _____   _____

End of Term — Percent attained: _____

Name _____

EXAMPLES OF REINFORCEMENT OPTIONS FOR ANGER-MANAGEMENT TRAINING

1. Have each student identify a success story in using one or more strategies in anger control. Have group members identify the strategy used in each case and give the student praise.

2. Identify ahead of time specific things you've observed each student do and say where you think they should be proud of growth and progress made in effort, internal responsibility, and anger control. Don't try to do this "off the cuff." Take time to prepare this ahead of class and then go around the circle with at least one item per student. Vary this activity, sometimes giving the feedback verbally and, at other times, writing these in "You should be proud" cards, inserting them in fortune cookies, or using some other means whereby the group members have this feedback in writing.

3. Have each student take time to identify and report growth they've observed in the person sitting next to them—that is, in exercising anger or depression management. This will take your leadership in order for it to be a powerful experience and may need to be done in several stages, as follows:

   a. Ask each student to share an anger-control goal they are willing to work on in the group; then have each student complete the Gift Card Pay to Group Members. Also, have each student negotiate an appropriate reward that the group will provide when she or he meets the anger-control goal. These rewards then can be transferred onto the Gift Certificates, which indicate that the reward will be paid to the bearer when she or he successfully meets the anger-control goal in Anger Management for Youth.

   b. Post the Gift Cards and Gift Certificates in the room.

   c. Ask for reports after a day or two and then again at the end of the week (or whatever period of time is negotiated by the group). Be firm during reports and do not let them get negative. Also, be prepared to provide additional evidence as needed if the observer is absent or needs assistance with his or her task. Distribute GIFT CERTIFICATES as earned.

4. Establish a "Bring and Brag" routine for the beginning of each group session. Put it on the agenda and ask, *"Does anyone have a Bring and Brag?"* This becomes a time when students can automatically report on and receive praise and applause for trying an anger-control strategy, experiencing a success, taking a hard step, and so forth.

NOTE:

Sprinkle skills-training and group-work sessions liberally with positive reinforcement of growth. Keep track of multiple ways of making reinforcement from you and the group both genuine and specific! This is the essence of *SOCIAL SUPPORT!*

References and Further Reading

Articles, Books and Pamphlets

Bandura, A (1973). *Aggression: A social learning analysis.* Englewood Cliffs, NJ: Prentice-Hall.

Bandura, A (1977). Self-efficacy: Toward a unifying theory of behavioral change. *Psychology Review, 84,* 191-215.

Bandura, A & Walters RH (1959). *Adolescent aggression: a study of the influence of child-training practices and family inter-relationships.* Bks Demand.

Bond, LA & Compas, BE (1989). *Primary Prevention & Promotion in the Schools.* Newbury Park: Sage.

Botvin, GJ & Dusenbury, L (1989). Substance abuse prevention and the promotion of competence. In *Primary Prevention & Promotion in the Schools* (pp. 146-178). Newbury Park: Sage.

Brendtro, LK, Brokenleg, M & Van Bockern, S (1990). *Reclaiming Youth at Risk.* Bloomington, IN: Natl Ed Serv.

Clarke, G (1990). Group cognitive-behavioral treatment of adolescent depression (Symposium). Conference for Reconnecting At-Risk Youth Project Team, Seattle, WA.

Clum, GA, Priester, M & Weaver, T et al. (1993). Group problem-solving and group support treatments for chronic suicide ideation. Paper presented at the 26th annual Am Assoc of Suicidology Conference. San Francisco, April.

Compas, BE, Phares, V & Ledoux, N (1989). Stress & coping preventive interventions for children & adolescents. In LA Bond & BE Compas (Eds), *Primary Prevention and Promotion in the Schools* (pp. 255-296). Newbury Park: Sage.

Conrath, J (1993). *Prevention Curriculum.* Lopez Island, WA.

Curtis, S (1992). Promoting health through a developmental analysis of adolescent risk behavior. *J School Health,* 62(9), 417-20.

Deffenbacher, JL (1988). Cognitive-relaxation and social skills treatment of anger: a year later. *J of Counseling Psychology,* 35(3), 234-36.

Deffenbacher JL & Stark, RS (1992). Relaxation and cognitive-relaxation treatments of general anger. *J of Counseling Psychology,* 39(2), 158-67.

Dorn, FJ (1984). The social influence model: A social psychological approach to counseling. *The Personnel & Guidance J,* 62(6), 342-45.

Dryfoos, J (1991a). Adolescents at risk: A summation of work in the field. Programs and policies. *J Adol Health,* 12(8), 630-37.

Dryfoos, J (1991b). Preventing high risk behavior. *Am J of Public Health,* 81(2), 157-58.

Eggert, LL (1985). Individual and group therapy with adolescents. In DL Critchley & JT Maurin (Eds) *The Clinical Specialist in Psychiatric Mental Health Nursing: Theory, Research and Practice* (pp. 198-228). NY: Wiley.

Eggert, LL (1990). Conducting intervention research with high-risk youth. *Comm Nurs Res,* 23, 175-82.

Eggert, LL & Herting, JR (1993). Drug exposure among potential dropouts and typical youth. *J Drug Ed,* 23, 31-55.

Eggert, LL & Herting, JR (1991). Preventing teenage drug abuse: exploratory effects of network social support. *Youth and Society,* 22, 482-524.

Eggert, LL, Nicholas, LJ, Owen, L & Associates (1993). *Personal Growth Class Groups: Leader's Guide.* Unpublished manual. Seattle, WA: University of Washington, SC-76, 98195.

Eggert, LL & Nicholas, LJ (1992). Speaking like a skipper: *"Skippin' an' gettin' high".* J Lang Soc Psy, 11, 75-100.

Eggert, LL, Herting, JR, Thompson, EA & Nicholas, LJ (June, 1992). *Reconnecting at-risk youth to prevent drug abuse, school dropout, suicide lethality.* Technical Report prepared and presented to the Advisory Council, NIMH.

Eggert, LL, Seyl, C & Nicholas, LJ (1990). Effects of a school-based prevention program for potential high school dropouts and drug abusers. *Int J Addictions,* 25, 772-801.

Eggert, LL, Thompson, EA, Herting, JR, Nicholas, LJ, Dicker, BG (1994). Preventing adolescent drug abuse and high school dropout through an intensive school-based social network development program. *American J. of Health Promotion,* 8(3), 1-14.

Furlong, MJ & Smith, DC (Eds) (1994). *Anger, Hostility and Aggression: Assessment, Prevention and Intervention Strategies for Youth.* Clinical Psych.

Glick, B. & Goldstein, AP (1987). Aggression replacement training. J. of Counseling & Development, 65(7), 356-62.

Goldstein, AP, Glick, B, *et al.* (1986). Aggression replacement training: a comprehensive intervention for the acting-out delinquent. *J. of Correctional Education,* 37(3), 120-26.

Goldstein, AP, Glick, B, Reiner, S, Zimmerman, D, Coultry, TM (1987). *Aggression Replacement Training: A Comprehensive Intervention for Aggressive Youth.* Research Press.

Goldstein, AP, Harootunian, B, & Conoley, J (1994). *Student aggression: prevention, control, replacement.* Guildford Pr.

Goldstein, AP & Pentz, M (1984). Psychological skill training and the aggressive adolescent. *School Psychology Review,* 13(3), 133-23.

Hazaleus, SL & Deffenbacher, JL (1986). Relaxation and cognitive treatments of anger. *J. of Consulting and Clinical Psychology,* 54(2), 222-26.

Hurrelman, K (1990). Health promotion for adolescents: Preventive and corrective strategies against problems behavior. *J of Adol,* 13(3), 231-50.

James J & Savary M (1977). *A New Self.* Reading, MA: Addison-Wesley.

Kaplan, RM, Konecni, VJ & Novaco, RW (Eds) (1983). *Aggression in Children and Youth.*

Kellam, SG (1990). Developmental epidemiological framework for family research on depression and aggression. In GR Patterson (Ed), *Depression and Aggression in Family Interaction* (pp. 11-48). Englewood Cliffs, NJ: Lawrence Erlbaum.

Kindler, HS (1988). *Managing Disagreement Constructively.* Los Altos, CA: Crisp Publications, Inc.

Leeman, LW, Gibbs, JC & Fuller, D (1993). Evaluation of a multi-component group treatment program for juvenile delinquents. *Aggressive Behaviors,* 19(4), 281.

Long, NJ (1991). What Fritz Redl taught me about aggression: Understanding the dynamics of aggression and counteraggression in students and staff. In *Crisis Intervention in Residential Treatment.* The Haworth Press.

Meichenbaum, DH & Deffenbacher, JL (1988). Stress inoculation training. *Counseling Psychologist,* 16(1), 69-90.

Meichenbaum, D (1977). *Cognitive-behavior modification, an integrative approach.* NY: Plenum Press.

Miller, WR & Rollnick, S (1991). *Motivational Interviewing.* NY: Guilford.

Miller, WR & Sanchez, VC (1993). Motivating young adults for treatment and lifestyle change. In G Howard (Ed), *Issues in Alcohol Use and Misuse by Young Adults.* Notre Dame, IN: U of Notre Dame Press.

National Institute of Mental Health (1990). *Research on Children & Adolescents with Mental, Behavioral & Developmental Disorders.* Washington, D.C.: US Dept of Health & Human Services.

Novaco, RW (1975). *Anger Control: The Development and Evaluation of an Experimental Treatment.* Lexington, Mass: Heath & Co.

Parens, H (1993). *Aggression in Our Children: Coping with It Constructively.* Aronson.

Quick, J, Francis, M, Hernandez, M, Earl, L & Friedman, RM (1980). *Appropriate Anger Expression Curriculum.* Adolescent Project, Child, Adolescent, and Community Program, Florida Mental Health Institute, 13301 North 30th Street, Tampa, FL. 33612.

Reaching Out: School-based Community Service Programs (1988). Washington, D.C.: Nat Crime Prev Council.

Schinke, SP & Gilchrist, LD (1984). *Life Skills Counseling with Adolescents.* Austin, TX: Pro-Ed.

Stone, EJ & Perry, CL (1990). United States: Perspectives in school health. *Journal of School Health, 60,* 363-68.

Tobler, NS (1986). Meta-analysis of 143 adolescent drug prevention programs. *J Drug Issues,* 16(4), 537-67.

Tosi, DJ (1974). *Youth: Toward Personal Growth.* Columbus, OH: Charles E. Merrill.

Vorrath, H & Brendtro, L (1985). *Positive Peer Culture* (2nd ed). Chicago: Aldine.

Wills, TA (1982). *Basic Processes in Helping Relationships.* NY: Academic Press.

Young, HS (1974). *A Rational Counseling Primer.* Institute for Rational Living, Inc., 45 East 65th Street, New York, NY 10021.

Assessment Scales

Corcoran, K & Fischer, J (1987). *Measures for Clinical Practice, A Source Book.* NY: The Free Press.

Freedman, B (1974). A Social-Behavioral Analysis of Skills Deficits in Delinquent and Non-Delinquent Adolescent Boys. [Doctoral dissertation]. University of Wisconsin, Madison.

Seigel, JM (1986). The multidimensional anger inventory. *Journal of Personality and Social Psychology,* 51(1), 191-200.

The POMS (Profile of Mood States) (1971). Educational and Industrial Testing Service, San Diego, CA 92107.

Thompson, EA & Leckie, M (1989). Interpretation manual for the symptoms of stress inventory. Unpublished manual. Seattle, WA: University of Washington.
Available from: Stress Management Clinic, Department of Psychosocial Nursing, SC-76, University of Washington, Seattle, WA 98195.
Attention: Dr. Elaine A. Thompson.

DID YOU KNOW THAT WE PROVIDE
STAFF DEVELOPMENT OPPORTUNITIES?

The National Educational Service has a strong commitment to enhancing the lives of youth by producing top-quality, timely materials for the professionals who work with them. Our resource materials include books, videos, and professional development workshops in the following areas:

Discipline with Dignity™

Working with Diverse Students

Reclaiming Youth at Risk™

Violence Prevention and Intervention

Catching Kids on the Edge

Conflict to Collaboration

Parents on Your Side

Our current mission focuses on celebrating diversity in the classroom and managing change in education.

NEED MORE COPIES OR ADDITIONAL RESOURCES ON THIS TOPIC?

Need more copies of this book? Want your own copy? Need additional resources on this topic? If so, you can order additional materials by using this form or by calling us at (800) 733-6786 or (812) 336-7700. Or you can order by FAX at (812) 336-7790.

We guarantee complete satisfaction with all of our materials. If you are not completely satisfied with any NES resource, just return it within 30 days and owe nothing.

Title	Price	Quantity	Total
Anger Management for Youth: Stemming Aggression and Violence	$22.95		
What Do I Do When...? How to Achieve Discipline with Dignity	$19.95		
Rediscovering Hope: Our Greatest Teaching Strategy	$19.95		
From Rage to Hope: Strategies for Reclaiming Black and Hispanic Students	$19.95		
Teaching in the Diverse Classroom: Learner-Centered Activities that Work	$19.95		
Safe Schools: A Handbook for Violence Prevention	$25.00		
Dealing with Youth Violence: What Schools and Communities Need to Know	$18.95		
Containing Crisis: A Guide for Managing School Emergencies	$19.95		
Breaking the Cycle of Violence (two-video set and Leader's Guide)	$325.00		
The Bullying Prevention Handbook	$21.95		
Discipline with Dignity (three-video set and Comprehensive Guide)	$445.00		
Shipping: Add 7% of order total, $3.00 minimum if check or credit card information is not included with your order.			

TOTAL _____

❏ Check enclosed with order   ❏ Please bill me (P.O. #_____)
❏ VISA or MasterCard   ❏ Money Order

Account No._____ Exp. Date_____
Cardholder Signature_____

SHIP TO:
Name_____ Title _____
Organization _____
Address_____
City_____ State_____ ZIP_____
Phone_____ FAX_____

MAIL TO:
National Educational Service
1252 Loesch Road
P.O. Box 8
Bloomington, IN 47402